Praise for *Swift*

"[David Baker] can lay down an elegant line when he wants to, but he favors an authenticating roughness to a consoling smoothness; when euphony and precision are at cross-purposes ⋯ ⋯riting, euphony yields. . . . All of Baker's poems are rich ⋯ ⋯, imagination and memory. But it's syntax that all⋯ ⋯ those elements, and to catch his own mi⋯

—E⋯ ⋯ *Book Review*

"[Baker] endows the land⋯ ⋯ and its wildlife with a cosmic radiance. . . . It wou⋯ ⋯rries around in his pocket a botanist's field guide, tucks u⋯ ⋯is arm a scrolled bundle of star charts that put the galactic whorls at his fingertips, and keeps well stocked a shelf of volumes cataloging every species from the *Asteroidea* to red-tailed hawks." —Floyd Collins, *Gettysburg Review*

"Baker is as thoughtful a poet as anyone writing today. It is as if his thoughts grew out of his sensations, not the other way around. The difference is a difference indeed, and *Swift* is a testament to its possibilities." —David Rigsbee, *Cortland Review*

"David Baker is a virtuoso of the long poem. . . . Meditative, ecological, and sensitively attuned to the complex interplay of subjectivity and context, *Swift* expands what it means for a self to be in conversation with larger systems. . . . The voice sustaining this collection is a sonorous whole." —Tyler Mills, *On the Seawall*

"David Baker is a master of places defined by science and art. . . . Baker grabs his audience with poems that are accurate yet creative, precise yet profound." —Andrew Jarvis, *New York Journal of Books*

"These are poems to read slowly as a place for sitting—to escape into a daily meditation where the good and the beautiful are filled with surprise. Baker uses the page in new and traditional ways. These implications from the earth make clear our societal issues and our personal relationships, and you will be grateful that someone is speaking for you." —Grace Cavalieri, *Washington Independent Review of Books*

"Opening the book, fifteen new poems invite us into an ecopoetic vision of subtlety as well as clarity. . . . If you're new to Baker's work as I was, expect to enjoy its formal permutations; couplets, fragments, thin columns and often full pentameter lines are all tools to build his aviaries. Thematically, the selected works evoke a naturalist's playful curiosity, a child's love for his parents, and a humanist's concern for the world." —Nate Duke, *Entropy*

"With each poem delicately and sturdily crafted, this collection creates one of the great spaces in American poetry."
—*Booklist*, starred review

" 'The soft pewter sky sets off the black / checkmark bodies of the birds as they skitter,' writes David Baker, and so background and foreground, stillness and motion are harnessed to describe an outer landscape that also delineates an inner, charged landscape. David Baker's new and selected poems reveal his keen imagination and the formal mastery that infuse his emotionally resonant work."
—Arthur Sze, National Book Award–winning author of *Sight Lines*

"No one writes with a more acute attention to the immediate world than David Baker, but his relish of particulars is always subject to a broader meditation that looks behind and ahead. If his large concern is nature, he should not be pigeonholed as an ecological or a pastoral poet. He is not only a poet of exacting, often scientific intelligence, but a poet of the heart. . . . To read the whole of *Swift* is to witness more than thirty years of exquisite artistry. David Baker is one of our finest poets."
—Rodney Jones, author of Pulitzer Prize finalist *Elegy for the Southern Drawl* and *Village Prodigies*

"*Swift: New and Selected Poems* gives us the exquisite ear of a poet laid over the precise eye of a naturalist. With Bishop's thick descriptive texture and Merwin's attention to vanishing, David Baker listens to the density of being. . . . Baker has the naturalist's intimacy with cycles of death and decay, but he is just as attentive to forces of disappearance in technology and contemporary life. The deep and sweeping power of these poems comes from showing us our own grief, our own loss of interconnectedness, and nature's capacity to offer us ways back into presence. They are full of everything I value most: humility, wonder, and a heartbreaking love for the world."

—Joanna Klink, author of *Excerpts from a Secret Prophecy*

swift

W. W. NORTON & COMPANY
Independent Publishers Since 1923

swift

New and Selected Poems

DAVID
BAKER

For information about permission to reproduce selections from this book, write to
Permissions, W. W. Norton & Company, Inc., 500 Fifth Avenue, New York, NY 10110

For information about special discounts for bulk purchases, please contact
W. W. Norton Special Sales at specialsales@wwnorton.com or 800-233-4830

Manufacturing by LSC Communications, Harrisonburg
Book design by JAM Design
Production manager: Lauren Abbate

Library of Congress Cataloging-in-Publication Data

Names: Baker, David, 1954– author.
Title: Swift : new and selected poems / David Baker.
Description: First edition. | New York : W. W. Norton & Company, [2019] | Includes
    bibliographical references and index.
Identifiers: LCCN 2018050859 | ISBN 9780393652765 (hardcover)
Subjects: LCSH: American poetry—20th century. | American poetry—21st century.
Classification: LCC PS3552.A4116 A6 2019 | DDC 811/.54—dc23
LC record available at https://lccn.loc.gov/2018050859

ISBN 978-0-393-35817-9 pbk.

W. W. Norton & Company, Inc., 500 Fifth Avenue, New York, N.Y. 10110
www.wwnorton.com

W. W. Norton & Company Ltd., 15 Carlisle Street, London W1D 3BS

1 2 3 4 5 6 7 8 9 0

for Page Hill Starzinger

  and Katherine Girard Baker

and in memory of Martha Baker

  and Donald Dayle Baker

Make mine Affections thy Swift Flyers neate . . .

Contents

ACKNOWLEDGMENTS   XV

NEW POEMS

Pastoral   3
Why Not Say   4
Early May   5
Stolen Sonnet   7
Why Not Say   9
Tree Frogs   10
The Sea   11
After   13
The Osprey   14
Waiting for News   16
The Wren   17
Gather   18
Checkpoint   19
Elegy, in Words   21
Peril Sonnet   22

from *SCAVENGER LOOP* (2015)

Swift   27
Simile   29
What Is a Weed?   30
Magnolia   33
Five Odes on Absence   34
Belong To   39
Scavenger Loop   41

from *NEVER-ENDING BIRDS* (2009)

Trillium   73
Posthumous Man   75

The Rumor 79

Horse Madness 82

Never-Ending Birds 85

Bay 86

Too Many 89

from *MIDWEST ECLOGUE* (2005)

Monarchs Landing and Flying 93

Hyper- 94

The Spring Ephemerals 98

Winged 100

Midwest Eclogue 101

The Blue 104

Late Pastoral 105

from *CHANGEABLE THUNDER* (2001)

Benton's Clouds 111

Pulp Fiction 114

Trees beside Water 116

After Rain 119

The City of God 120

Unconditional Election 122

Ohio Fields after Rain 123

from *THE TRUTH ABOUT SMALL TOWNS* (1998)

Still-Hildreth Sanitorium, 1936 127

Yellow Lilies and Cypress Swamp 130

Holiday Bunting 132

The Truth about Small Towns 134

Tract 137

The Affair 139

Treatise on Touch 140

from *AFTER THE REUNION* (1994)

Snow Figure	145
Along the Storm Front	147
Red Shift	148
Faith	150
Murder	151
Mercy	156
After the Reunion	157

from *SWEET HOME, SATURDAY NIGHT* (1991)
and *HAUNTS* (1985)

November: The End of Myth	161
Starlight	162
Patriotics	164
Running the River Lines	166
The Wrecker Driver Foresees Your Death	167
The Anniversary of Silence	169
Haunts	171
NOTES	175

Acknowledgments

The new poems here first appeared in the following journals, to whose editors I extend my grateful acknowledgment: *American Poetry Review*: "Why Not Say (1)," "Why Not Say (2)"; *The Atlantic*: "The Wren"; *Boston Review*: "Tree Frogs"; *Field*: "Early May"; *Five Points*: "Gather," "Waiting for News"; *The Nation*: "The Osprey"; *Poem-a-Day* (Academy of American Poets): "The Sea"; *Poetry*: "Peril Sonnet"; *T Magazine* (*New York Times*): "Pastoral"; *Tin House*: "After," "Elegy, in Words," "Stolen Sonnet." "Checkpoint" was published concurrently in the *Bennington Review* and *The Eloquent Poem* (Persea Books).

I am grateful also to Denison University for support and encouragement, and to Jill Bialosky for her abiding guidance and care.

*

New Poems

Pastoral

Here at the center	of a field	of green
leaves waving	center of a	grief I can't
see far enough	to tell how	it will ease
it will not ease	it goes on	and on now
as yours does	in sunlight	and in rain
holding hands with	her in the	last minutes
sky so vast	hear the	wheat roar—

Why Not Say

What happened. This terrible breaking, this blow. Then slow
    the dogwood strewn like tissue along the black road.
No the busy pollinators the breeze in the pine shadows
    in the aftermath where I drove back there. And two bones
of smoke lifting ahead along the shoulder in the high new
    green weed-bank running beside the asphalt. No
I had come from my father. Nothing more common nothing more
    than such. I could not breathe for the longest time
over and again. There was something deadly, she said, in it.
    Of the genus *Buteo*, as *B. harlani*, as Harlan's red-tail.
Blocky in shape, goes the book, blood or brick-red but white
    I am sure underneath, white along its wing, which was not smoke
but rising now one bird. I was coming back and couldn't breathe
    and him bruised torn bedridden tubed taken to the brink
by his body and carried aloft. There he had fallen.
    This is what happened said the medical team. Fallen:
and ripped aortal stenosis in the process of their repair.
    No the white bird strained, as trying to lift, to a *slight*
dihedral, the deepest deliberate wing beats, and barely
    above the snow-white-lipped grasses and the shoulder
until I thought I would hit it. It happened or
    it did not, in the way of my thinking. And now why
I saw. Two lengths of snake helical and alive in the talons
    heavy there, writhing, so the big bird strained for the length
of time that it takes. Like the oiled inner organs
    of a live thing heaving in shreds, the dogwoods
the doctors, and did I say the horrible winds all before.
    Now the air after storm. The old road empty. Swept white,
by blossoms by headlights, my father hovering still:
    why it flew so close, why it was so terribly slow.
I think I hoped it would tear me to pieces. Lift me,
    of my genus *helpless*, as *wretched*. And drop me away.
I turned back to the animal. No it turned its back to me.

Early May

It's torn apart

like a white reef no

petals over the yard

that kind of mist

this morning but how

bright as a clot in

those high green limbs

if you open one chunk

"inconspicuous"

by an involucre

like bracts he *broke*

chunk of coral and

more than fourteen

worms belonging to

different species

more than morning mist

it's all coming apart

is that dogwood first

no it is not

I mean white canopy

gorgeous a red bird

the dogwood beneath

it's all coming apart

of it small heads

flowers surrounded

of pale petal-

apart this volleyball-sized

found living inside

hundred *polychaete*

103

how did we lose it

we don't call it

extinction we never had it like

white siding peeling off the barn's sun side

like smoke no a white shelf no fog of wild-

fires chewing through California searing

the rain forests pushing up from acid

vents far below the white urchins dying

we talk about it what color gets this

right in the backyard *as "biotic attrition"*

on the canopy it's been tea for fevers

poultice of cornus tannin for wounds

and berries after "slight bletting" for jam

estivate of what- ever we might do

are we too late blood bone salty leafing

star motes hurrying going down through the

floating now green canopy white petals

is that snow—

Stolen Sonnet

And when my life is
over [hush he said]—

     *

Take this statue take
these wings   my coat—

     *

Look the robins have
come back to the crab—

     *

[where is that he said]—

[where are—he said—we]—

     *

too   *a distant bell*
too   a distant bell—

     *

There's something [he wrote]
I want you to do—

     *

Feeding on frozen
apples
        all there is—

*

Will you please put it
back where you got it—

*

The hawk's shadow hunts
the chipmunk's shadow—

*

Her cramped hand   "seeds for
little white flowers"—

*

And stars that fell like
rain out of the blue—

*

Keep singing   until
the song is no more—

*

[see the pyramids]

we were together—

*

Which is I stood and
loved you while you slept—

Why Not Say

What happened. We brought his walker. The shallows. The heat.
   The matted grasses and river willows re-greening
the hard mudbanks. From the new bridge the old bridge.
   I helped him out of the car. Left him there to park the car
at the broken gate going to the fallow fields, the car there
   where we had walked another life the plowed furrows,
picking up arrowheads. Funnels of swallows in a swirl risen
   from the trestle beneath us and many low limbs.
What a racket, he said, above us. Below us the old bridge
   footer of concrete, twisted ironworks, some shadows there.
What happened. He couldn't recall. In the night
   getting a box of pictures to hold on to. So he fell. So
we threw a few rocks. The high water low water again.
   Backwash and foam in the flood pools—no fault,
she said, there never is, the simple white gravel
   scattered on the new bridge surface and this time
he didn't fall. We went to the other side. What
   about that, he said. He threw a rock. The permanent
havoc of little mistakes. A hip full of pins and
   surgery scars. The hit-spit of a bluegill the cotton-
wood seeds small branches greening the old shoe eddying swallows
   the heat. The shallows. And the slow wash of days—

Tree Frogs

One starts. The still heat is a blown curtain.
The curtain wavers then—now two of them—

and another from beyond the blue agave.
Soon the whistling, *wheet-eet-eet*, the many,

so many tree frogs "no bigger than thumbprints,"
Eleutherodactylus coqui, the common coqui,

which we've never seen but in books, not once.
Now the purring, the rolling coo of

the mourning dove song of the island toads
among the hundred frogs, and crickets, Gryllidae,

in late day rising salt background waves,
as, in the bay, the small squall we didn't see

at first is a gray-bellied cloud in the still
yet azure twilight sky, and the container ship

pulls on through the sheath of mist—
a distant bell among the white cedars.

Can the ending of things ever be heard?
So slowly it crawls with the gross weight

of all our needs, our goods, our ghosts.
Such little things we are, and so much noise.

The Sea

urchins spread. They want enough room
on the seabed, along the black basaltic
jet of offshore reef, sun-pied, outswept, or
down along the darker overcrowded

urchin barrens, to quiver their hundred-
plus spines and not encroach or be encroached
or preyed upon, pulled, ripped apart by the
wolf eel, the next-to-deadliest lurking

shadow in these waters. Are more black
than not, and move, when they move, "by means of
tiny, transparent, adhesive tube feet"
by the hundreds. Though they prefer to stay.

The barrens are their own creation. Such
hunger, such efficient self-replication,
they tend to nullify what other lives
would abound in other seas. Black dandelions,

they're like a small explosion stilled; or
like that red-bloomed scrub bush in the cactus
gardens near our house, more scarlet than red,
whose name we haven't learned, flaring at each

air-breath like hair, so soft yet erect in
the afternoon burn like underwater
shimmers of the urchins themselves, lit red.
And red your foot—within a minute of

your step and cry—we tried to heal with cool
seawater poured over; and scrubbed the four
last snapped-off spines; then sat there on the shore.
Three boats went by. A yacht. The island

ferry hauling all the day's workers home.
Then, come night, was that a liner or our
local trash scow, far out, low-lit? You can see
the phosphorescent wake five miles from space.

After

1.

We came to the island. We stayed in the house.
Rain and sun. Bougainvillea. Pink cedar.
How many shadows slipped along walls
or whetted the leaves of century plants?

2.

We saw clouds from the windows. Far boats.
You left the bed and came back shaking.
Your mother, her white hair, or something
whose shape would never, at last, find you.

3.

Night palms clattering like hungry bowls.
Crazy whistling of the island peepers.
We walked to the water. Walked back.
We walked to the water . . . walked back.

The Osprey

or sea-eagle,
what the guidebook says is
white, grayish brown, and "possessed of weak eye-
masks" in its nonmigratory island

instance, is blue.
Blue, riding thermal bands
so low over the water it picks up
the water's color, reticulate

tarsi tipping
the light crests; and picks up
one of the silver fish cutting the surface
there, so the fish is blue, too, flapping-gone-

slack in the grasp
of its claws—as only
the owl shares an outer reversible
toe-talon, turned out for such clutching;

as the water,
in turn, picks up the sky-
depth reflective blue sent down from ages
beyond, into which the osprey lifts now

without a least
turning of wing-chord though
"they are able to bend the joint in their
wing to shield their eyes from the light"; what I

mean is, by the
time I tell you this it's
gone: fish-and-bird, away, "bone-breaker," brown
or gray "diurnal raptor," back into

the higher trades. Someday, too, this blue—

Waiting for News

Frigate overhead, riding the thermals,
    circling the bay. Mist beyond. And then
    the cargo steamer in a stitch of sunlight.
Look at it and it is mist.

From shore we've learned to glance aside to see
    the details of the sea. A degree, or two,
    there's a sail, the yellow harbor marker—
a neighbor's light across

the bay in haze. Cloud landscape of a cliff.
    We're waiting for word of loss that hasn't
    fallen yet, but due—. Is that gardenia,
or the little bird named

for bananas? Sometimes I see sorrow
    standing next to you. A paper bag prepared
    with weights. Salt urn. Her body powdery
as cloud. Now the white shirts

on the line below our house fill again,
    with wind, as though the body is a wind.
    The body is a wind. I look at you.
I see the sea. The sea is you.

The Wren

First it flies to a side rail. Then a fern.
Then a fern, like a fountain, spilling out.
   Can a curse be said to be song? Can it?
How can such a quick thing, tail tipped-up, brown
   as a bun, on wings too busy to see,
be so badly named? Troglodytidae.
   The term circles back to us—cave-dweller,
brute recluse. Though a wren's beak curves, like a
   scimitar, this one just wants its porch back.
Now it's vanished down our hollow eave-spout
   from whose depths returns—says the book—a *loud
and often complex song.* No, it is a curse.

Gather

This is what happened. I was with the tree. Come to gather
from the tree its heavy fruits, scent of far spices and filament
of fine brown cilia, a nubbled skin the color of new apples.
But heavy as stones these fruits. Bright green to lumine a room.
Or, in a bag, in a basement, enough to make spiders turn back
toward rain or new winter sifting down. I was with this tree.
Then my face was against this soil. Or an age passed, or a life.
I don't know. But I know now not to breathe is the better
to be with the breath of the others for a while. Felt them there,
the millions moving beneath my cheek, a taste of endlessness,
layers of leaves breaking down, moss twigs. Lay in the earth
and it filled my nose back into breath. Hedge apple and locust
had twirled together so I climbed one. Found there the other.
I didn't know then but one thorn had pierced my hand, clean
through. Another the meat of my calf falling. I waited, when
I woke, like a spider afloat. Wings of the shadow overhead.
Or in its over-brightness a revelation I had not known, had
not sought. Now there were songs with me starting again
among the heights resettling. I was not, I knew, nailed
to this body forever but a borrowed wind. Aroma of so
many with me always now at my cheek, more gathering—

Checkpoint

These are the days when birds come back.

These are the days the birds. These days

these birds. These days are these birds.

Let us see these days these papers. When

are these birds, and where are your papers.

Where are you going. Come back answer

me where you are going. Behind the barn,

the flame tree, our fire, our wings, these birds,

behind the trees the bursting winds the birds.

These days come back. They do not, there

what color is your ruby-throat, your toothbrush

yellow-breasted warbler green flame blue-

jay marsh thrush among the light the lush, low

timid leaf she said by the river what fire

is your nova is your wife's hairbrush

take off your shoes take your hands off

stop right there so many coming over as

so many millions fewer wings these papers

of fragile bones vanished they are not

where are you going I said come back.

Elegy, in Words

And then everything unfastened—. Did the wind.
    Was it wind. Was it in the pines, or the window.
Were they beyond where they were before. Where
    was that. Barn owl. I know. Like a whisper, only
lower; whimper, lower. Nothing hurt, but something
    beckoning, and very near. You won't believe this.
Nothing like *who cooks for you* of the barred owl.

He was humming. And the coyote, calling back,
    her whelps yipping back, and the wood-pipe calling
of the close bird kept on—is that how you can tell.
    No. I would have slept through. They'd
be maybe fifty yards off the rock ridge running
    beyond the pines. Not church, not
birthdays. He never sang, not one note.

He played a finger game—squeezing. I'd been there
    all day for days, like that, him humming. Gave
him a touch of bourbon to his lip, with a straw,
    what a face. He wanted—. No, I burned him.
I can't tell you how long, but they kept on calling
    each other out there in the pines. Then the phone.
That's the last he said to me in words. I can't imagine.

Peril Sonnet

Where do you suppose
                they've gone the bees now

that you don't see them
                anymore four-winged

among flowers low
                sparks in the clover

even at nightfall
                are they fanning have

they gone another
                place blued with pollen

stuck to their bristles
                waiting beyond us

spring dwindle is what
                we call it collapsing

neonicotinoids
                "high levels in pneu-

matic corn exhaust"
                loss of habitat

or *disappearing*
                disease in the way

of our kind   so to speak
                what do you think

they would call it

                language older than

our ears were they

                saying it all along

even at daybreak—

from

Scavenger Loop

Swift

1.

into flight, the name as velocity,
a swift is one of two or three hundred
swirling over the post office smokestack.
First they rise come dusk to the high sky,

flying from the ivy walls of the bank
a few at a time, up from graveyard oaks
and backyards, then more, tightening to orbit
in a block-wide whirl above the village.

2.

Now they are a flock. Now we're holding hands.
We're talking in whispers to our kind, who
stroll in couples from the ice cream shop
or bike here in small groups to see the birds.

A voice in awe turns inward; as looking
down into a canyon, the self grows small.
The smaller swifts are larger for their singing,
the spatter and high *cheeep*, the shrill of it.

3.

And their quick bat-like alternating wings.
And the soft pewter sky sets off the black
checkmark bodies of the birds as they skitter
like water toward a drain. Now one veers,

dives, as if wing-shot or worse out of the sky
over the maw of the chimney. Flailing—
but then pulling out, as another dips
and the flock reverses its circling.

4.

They seem like leaves spinning in a storm,
blown wild around us, and we their witnesses.
Witness the way they finish. The first one
simply drops into the flue. Then four,

five, in as many seconds, pulling out of
the swirl, sweep down. So swiftly, we're alone.
The sky is clear of everything but night.
We are standing, at a loss, within it.

Simile

1.

Orange-and-midnight the moth on the fringe tree—
first it nags a bloom; sips and chews; then shakes
the big flower. Then its wings slow. Grows
satiate, as in sex. Then still, as the good sleep after.
Each bloom a white torch more than a tree's flower.
Each is one of ten or twelve, conic, one of many
made of many green-white or white petals
held out, as by a hand, from the reach of the limb.
A field this morning was full of white moths. More
in the side yard, in the bluebottle, lifting—fog
off the dew, white wings like paper over flames
and floating awry or pieces of petal torn off.
Weeks now my words on paper have burned.
Burned and flown, like a soul on fire, with
nothing to show but ash, and the ash flies, too.

2.

Today, in the news—so many martyrs—
an "unnamed suicide bomber" took herself into
the arms of flame, and five others, "by her own hand."
Whitman means the beauty of the mind is terror.
Do you think I could walk pleasantly and
well-suited toward annihilation?
But there is no likeness beyond her body
in flames, for its moment, no matter its moment.
Yet the fringe bloom burns. Yet the moth shakes
and chews, as in sex. When the young maple
grows covered with seeds, they are a thousand
green wings, like chain upon chain of keys,
each with its tiny spark trying the black lock.
A tumbler turns and clicks. The world once more
fills with fire, and the body, like ash, is ash.

What Is a Weed?

1.

Emerald, as in the leaf of the ash,
though nothing's burned, not yet, as the ash-green,
gray-green fiery wingspan of the adult
whose bullet body and flat black eyes are
less the way we know them than by the trees,
by the death of the trees, by the millions.
The adults emerge, *A. planipennis*
(of the genus *Agrilus*), in May, June,
July, then in bark crevices, between
layers of the diamond derma, females
set their eggs whose larvae, in a week, bore
back into the trees. They chew the phloem.
They eat the inner body of the bark,
creating winding galleries as they feed.
This "cuts the flow" of water nutrients
to the tree. This "causes dieback," causes death.

2.

What is a weed? What I saw was a tree.
A thousand trees in the village, more, but
one at the point of the street corner lot
where all summer I held my girl by the back
of her bike and ran the green block down.
The tree was obvious, catalpa, its long
three-branching trunks splayed like a birch, whose
shagbark white parchment skin is equally
unmistakable—leaves as big as a
piece of paper, if the page were a heart
or head of a spade, and pale green, foot-long-at-
least bean pods dangling like ropy toys—

three trunks pushing from our one earth, equally
thick, the same height. And then, among two trunks
of waving catalpa, I saw ash leaves, fist-
sized but delicate, blooming from the third.

3.

All over the village the ashes are
dying. Already dead, my tree friend says.
The scourge emerald borer rode in on
shipping crates, Asia via Lake Erie,
2002. They date it to the month.
And in bundles of firewood, in luggage
of travelers, in bedding plants, their radiant
splay spread "like wildfire," up Ontario,
down, through Ohio, Illinois . . . and now
7.5 billion ash trees, mountain
white (*Fraxinus americana*) and blue,
fragrant, Carolina, green, (family of
Oleaceae), of opposite branching,
of compound pinnate leaf, whose timber is
"wonderfully springy," excellent for oars
and tools, "and lends itself to steaming and

4.

turning," as in bentwood furniture, will die.
Though some refer to them as trash. Trash ash.
What is a weed? And the answerer says
a plant that doesn't fit the local plan.
In my personal doctrine of signatures
you can tell the emerald ash borer
simply by its hole, the letter D, as
it emerges from the host—each circle
with its flattened edge or side—a hundred
or more, like buckshot, on a tree sometimes,

or on a tree braided to another tree.
Two catalpas growing with a third.
I pushed my daughter down the street, let go,
and her laughter lit the waiting trees—ash
or trash, catalpa, oak . . . the neighborhood
where she learned to fly. Then the trees grew wings.

Magnolia

We were done for. Things broken. Things ugly.
   It being the shut end of night. Morning breaking, more
like a bruise smeared through the wet few uppermost leaves.
   Not yet light so much as less dark. They shouldn't grow
this far north. That's what the book says. What book.
   What I meant was, each day begins in the dark.
That's useless that's too late that's a pathetic thing to say—
   older than bees the magnolia. More primitive, the book
says, whose carpels are extremely tough. They do not flower
   in sepals. They do not want such differentiation
in their flower parts, from whence the term tepals.
   They open, the anthers, splitting themselves out. That's your
melodrama. No they split at the front facing the flower center.
   16-something. Pierre Magnol. Morning starting through them
like a purple bruise, then a cloud, one small pale blue
   stretchmark, another, then another. That's not right.
Flowers developed to encourage pollination by beetles. Too
   early for bees. Grew tough to avoid damage by said beetles.
—There you have it. *Magnolia virginiana*. Subfamily
   Magnolioideae of the family Magnoliaceae.
Relations have been puzzling taxonomists for a long time—
   to survive ice ages, tectonic uptearing, slow drift
of the continents, a distribution scattered. Things too old
   for change, mutinous in the half-light, and malignant.
Stop it please please. They shouldn't be this far north.
   They bloom in a cup of pink fire, each one, lit by an old oil.
Before us the bees. Before us the bees the beetles. These trees
   —so what. We had walked out earlier, the porch, late
terrible dark night. Their natural range a disjunct dispersal.
   No light. The magnolia. The eye begins to see. Then the long
horrible scrape on its trunk, his single stretching paring
   of the bark back. But he didn't finish his discomfort, his
antler velvet a cloud of sawdust and scrapings beneath like
   small remains of a cold fire. All night trying, then no
longer trying, that's when we walked out. He must have run.

Five Odes on Absence

1.

    M Drst, he starts, *M nrl wrn t . . .*

And if purple's the new black as the mag
says (according to their latest ad-tweet,
it s the seasons thing), perhaps erasure's
our poetry du jour. At the Walker
contemporary poets have been
composing "astounding new work" by
removing portions of existing . . .

    Nbd wll wn M r hv m . . . & wht hv dn . . .

"Join us as several guest poets read from
and display their latest or landmark e-
rasures." Which means: take Dickinson, rub
some letters out, you can be famous, too.
Because I could not stop for Death—make that
Be a cold sop. I stood at—. You get the
picture. Sappho: without time's injury.

    ppl tll m hv gt n hm n ths wrld . . .

2.

My neighbor's boy Bernard is practicing.
Bang against his father's garage, painted
a week ago, taupe siding and light brown
sliding doors trimmed out and edged in white.

Bang and three dozen grackles scatter off
the ornamental crab where they had lit.

Beautiful tree to be so full of birds.
Beautiful birds whose shape maintains a tree

when they disperse, silhouette widening
like a flower blooms, or limbs in blue flight.
Bang and his skates scrape down the concrete drive.
He taps his stick—he digs his rollers in—

Bernard's usually dead-eyed with a puck
but wild today. *Thwack*. Paint puff. One more scar
on the door where he's missed the net once more.
That's his father watching from the window.

That's his mother not there, not there, not there—

3.

Mr. Clare wants a little privacy.
Who can blame him? It's 1849.
All his life he's tried to get words right—
                    hurried
The startld stockdove ~~hurriying~~ wizzing bye
                    the sky
As the still hawk hangs oer ~~him~~ in dusk
                    as they
Crows from the oaks trees qawking ~~flusk~~ spring
~~*Wafting the stillness of the woods*~~—

get the birds right. Or the trees. It's not code
exactly. Now he's the talkative in-
mate/patient of Northamptonshire County
General Lunatic Asylum; and
now he's boxed with gipsies, written *Don
Juan*, lived on grass one mad escape home
and yet thou art not there. And now he writes

to Mary Collingwood (is she Mary
Bolland? is she Patty?) *Drst Mr
r fthfll r d thnk f m* . . . pulling
out the vowels, *dd vst me n hll,*
leaving out the y's, *sm tm bck . . . flsh
ppl tll m hv gt n hm n ths wrld* . . .
Who can blame him? He gets confused,

                              hope
weaving it this way. *Is faded all ~~a thought~~.*
He lived in a house with seven children,
whr r th . . . He was the rage of London,
peasant poet, friend of . . . *whr r th* . . .
Some days now he pulls weeds to keep busy,
though his doctors want him inside, enclosed
for safety's sake. He sings them little songs.

I am—yet what I am, none cares or knows;
My friends forsake me like a memory lost:
I am the self-consumer of my woes.
3000 plus poems in a lifetime,
not code exactly, not exactly not.
bt dnt cm hr gn fr t s
ntrs bd plc . . . rs fr vr & vr
                              Jhn Clr

4.

Morandi paints a bottle by painting
everything around the bottle but not
the bottle. This is how it always is.
Wherever I am I am what is missing.
Twiteren: bird song; tremble; high-pitched laughter;
state of great agitation; quiver; ~~eye~~
I feel I am—I only know I am
And plod upon the earth as dull and void:

The keyword is verisimilitude.
It's not enough to tell the truth; you have
to tell it in believable fashion.
Then buyers won't care what you omit—
Earth's prison chilled my body with its dram
Of dullness and my soaring thoughts destroyed.
Twittering is writing messages of
140 characters or less,
no matter the message, using @Twitter.
These are live updates of what one's doing.
I fled to solitudes from passion's dream.
But now I only know I am—that's all.

5.

Some days Isaac sits on the deck all day.
He holds his head. He drinks a lot. He weeps.
The birds are landing black, then purple, as
the sun picks up the oils on their wings.
The heavy crab grows heavier with them.
The pink blossoms grow shivery, like wings.
I understand the patience. Sometimes I do.

I wonder what Bernard sees when he sees
the open net yawning there. Toward the end
Morandi painted fewer lines—bigger
ghosts. Made an edge with a sketch of edges
behind the pale line of each edge. That's all
it takes, innuendo of a thing, the way,
bang, now the grackles explode out again

in a crazy puff of wings. Bernard's rage
is the hard pink downfall of petals there,
or not there, as he skates back down the drive.
I sit with my magazines and cell phone.
I feel crazy drifting by myself.

Sometimes I think the birds are shadows of
some other thing—I just can't see it well—

black, then purple, then purple turning black.
You get the picture. On a better day
Clare writes, the starnels darken down the sky.
But that's the price of time's erasure, too,
sad memories of a happier life.
Ppl mk sch mstks. It isn't code . . .
whr r . . . Then what he doesn't write is you.

Belong To

See the pair of us
>   *Raining and morning*

the first soft ashes
>   along the high road

running the far ridge
>   of pines ripped wild to

timbers by storming
>   to shreds see the white

shreds *like coals* like a
>   sudden sorrow see

the partial moon see
>   the cut sky see us

serene with singing
>   are we merry are

we rueful neither
>   is there sufficient

wording for what falls
>   *all the muffled horns*

pleading but too late
>   along the last route

of what remains can
                you see us what can

you see there—*lost leaves*
                waiting to come back

as leaves—

Scavenger Loop

Buddy, can I dig?
But he's already
    deep into it, pile I've dragged
    all morning, piece by piece, to the curb.

He's a seasoned picker
—I can tell—his CRV backed up
    right to the rubble and
    hatchback popped open, half-full, at 9 a.m., of

whatnots and what-ifs: heirloom
silver in a hand-tooled box, a baby's clothes, books
    in bright wrappers.
    He's come from a county away

to score—his term—whatever he can
the day before
    our village "free-for-haul"
    is officially underway.

In the wild, animals lie where they die, thus placing them into the
scavenger loop. The upshot is that the highly concentrated animal
nutrients get spread over the land, by the exodus of flies, beetles, etc.

•

You need to get home as soon as you can.
The doctor thinks you should come back, *right now*—

•

Dustscaewung . . . a kind of daydream of dust, a pondering of that
which has been lost: dust-*seeing*, dust-*chewing*, dust-*cheering.* The
daydream of a mind strung between past and present.

Row on row of rich green stalks.

•

Something is coming more than we know how.

An hour ago on Facebook one newly
friended friend posted: Repeal Monsanto
Protection Act, as it "deregulates
the GMO industry from any
court oversight." This status update was
"shared" from a status update which picked it
from someone else's status, and so on.
Seventy-seven people "like" this post—
a record for me, my new friend comments
in the comment box of her own update.
A complex and mobile intimacy . . .

.

as in old woods, as
dies, and starts to rot,
for decades. "More than
species depend on
both for their food and
The body decays and
"specialist beetles"
tiny tastes of nu-
their burrows, maybe
millimeters wide,"
sawdust as they chew:
tinder polypore,
The wood returns to

when a single tree
yet it may remain
a third of the bird
standing dead trees,
for nesting places."
the larvae of some
process the wood for
tritious starch inside—
only "one to three
spill a powdery
powderpost, deathwatch,
sulfur shelf, sapsucker—.
the soil as humus.

The road out of town . . .
                    and always the same road
back—

The USDA projected 2013 US corn production at 14,140 million
bus, based on the Prospective Plantings number of 97.3 million acres
planted, 8% average abandonment resulting in harvested area of
89.5 million acres, and an average yield of 158 bus an acre.

•

I am her son   *sign here*   She's my mother

•

I am up to a hundred "likes" OMG

•

Apologizes to the doctor   for dying—

Cessation of the furosemide *loop
diuretic*, cessation of O_2—

      •

That's a pacemaker not a defib who—

      •

She sang "Yellow Bird" when she was happy—

      •

1 farmer :: 151 consumers
farm and ranch families < 2%
of the national population—

      •

Her mysteries her bells her soaps her coats—

      •

Didn't this used to be Johnny's Sinclair?—

      •

When I asked what she needed—water—soup—
she said *Seven-up*   *tiramisu!*—

      •

*When we reduce biodiversity by breaking up the forest for our
backyards, we accidentally free undiluted disease organism[s]
to operate at full strength . . .*

You may not be tired but I'm tired—

Night sky so vast   hear the wheat roar—

SmartStax RIB Complete, a single bag refuge
solution against earworm, army worm.

Row on hundreds of rows of rich green stalks—
knee high by the 4th of July and eight

feet or more before the fall—Monsanto
"offers corn farmers the ability

to control weeds and pests with a single
seed through a process known as 'trait stacking.'"

Thus DroughtGard Hybrids, VT Triple PRO
for above-ground insect protection stacked with

below-ground rootworm protection and Round-
Up Ready 2 Technology to fight

Goss's Wilt, Gray Leaf Spot, chronic drought, corn
borer . . .

•

                              rummaging each other's trash heaps—

•

We deny that we are animals and part of the wheel of life, part
of the food chain. We deny that we are part of the feast and
seek to remove ourselves from it, even though we kill and
consume animals by the billions and permanently remove the
life resources for many more. But not one animal is allowed to
consume us, even after we are dead. Not even the worms.

Give him some money   Is it muddy there

is it Four up five up six up seven

up seven up   Can we go now   I want

to go now please   David some money   Please

is it nice is it muddy is it some

money   Sweet the   Hmm   Hmm   Let's go today

I want to go   Tomorrow   Sun   Today

What can you see already from the chair

Is it   Bubbles I like them   Must can we go

Hmm   Eight up nine up eleven twelve—

David Philip Dayle David Philip Dayle

those are my men   What can you see now

oh grace the Come on   Come now   Oh no my

is it muddy honey awful I'm not—

I'm just a picker, he says.
It's a hobby, not subsistence. *Leastways not*
    hereabouts. Treasure hunter,
    geocacher, scrounge . . .

    •

skawage, Middle English :: customs—as from

escauwage, Old North French :: inspection—as from

scēawian, Old English :: to look at—or lately

with some "semantic drift," English :: show—

    •

decomposers and detritivores complete the process by consuming
remains left by scavengers—

She was fifteen
maybe, riding her bike those long evenings
down old AA where it all turned blacktop
and gravel past the Lindsey place farther
than the quarry pool. Evening fireflies
above the soybeans. Swallows in the air.
She was never in a hurry. Once in

a little sprinkle she pulled off the road
and we saw slung over her back wheel like
saddlebags a cluster of plastic milk-
cartons she used riding around to tweak
her product. A week later her huffer-
chef-boyfriend blew up their stove and him with it.
She didn't die though her forehead melted

and a few fingers fighting it off and
her hair, part of one ear, top lip, you know,
lucky girl. Row on row by the thousands
of tall stalks growing so straight they seem combed,
every twenty rows a seed sign to mark
varietals of the labs' latest tests,
Agrigold 6267 Agrigold 6472 . . .

Peck baskets line the

       market sidewalk packed

with local apples

       the sheriff's running

more folks off for

       loitering so the streets

are quiet nights

       so much depends

on what they

       tell you for your

patronage or vote

       so much more

as malathion

       in the skin on what

they don't—

·

Come, kill the Worm, that doth its kirnell eate
    And strike thy sparkes within my tinderbox.

·

An average of nine different fungicides and pesticides
discovered in bee pollen are tied to Colony Collapse Disorder—

·

Who would I show it   *so unprocessed* to—

Her letter, started years ago, leaving
Evelyn's pie safe. Waterford bells.

Grandmother's thimbles her material.
How do you keep a thing you cannot touch?

Agrigold 6376.
Portrait of the boys above the table.

Denbeigh Acres Our Manors Have Manners.
Four names. One crossed out. Heirlooms edited.

Quilts towels Mother hand-stitched some linens
pillowcases   [   ]   FOPs tolerant.

Walk around and stick a yellow Post-it
on the stuff you want is what he told me.

Nutcracker Kitchen—cornbread from heaven.
14 China Birds. Publix Cineplex.

International Harvester. Archer
Daniels Midland, Tyson, ConAgra, Swift . . .

The world gives you itself in fragments / in splinters:

•

The grey lawns cold where gold, where quickgold lies!
　　Wind-beat whitebeam! airy abeles set on a flare!
　　Flake-doves sent floating forth at a farmyard scare!
Ah well! it is all a purchase, all is a prize.

•

['splɪn tər]

•

n.
a very small sharp piece of wood, glass, metal, etc., characteristically
long and thin

　　　　　　　broken off from the main body;

(Military, Firearms, Gunnery, Ordnance & Artillery) a metal fragment,
from the container of a shell, bomb, etc., thrown out during explosion;

splinter group, separate factions, sect; as of church, as of family;

obs. secured by splint or splints—

vb.
to reduce or be reduced to sharp fragments;

shatter;

break off in small shards—

Tell me, where does it hurt? *Everywhere else—*

—broken shutters, musty box
springs, two ancient-at-
    eight-years-old laser printers
    and all manner of lawnmowers, power tools, hand

tools, shredded planters, to name only a bit
of the stuff crammed
    in my barn: as for me,
    fewer loves, yet more

amassed . . . as there, out
behind the barn, the pile of waterlogged lumber
    where the new fawns
    this spring were born, and farther yet, between

oak leaf hydrangeas and scrub trees
I've thinned out
    for cosmetic sake, for fewer leaves to rake,
    for more sun, thick grass (thus

the complexity of the whole
system diminished:
    another *positive feedback loop* lost)—
    there, beyond

the village's big houses,
there, past nail parlors,
    the franchise hardware shop, fast-food shacks
    and tattoo sheds,

beyond the strips, the burbs,
there, the sunken barns
    where row on row
    the fields spread, running out through the country,

the corn fields, the soy beans,
for ten miles, a hundred
　　　more, for
　　　a thousand miles of *rich green stalks* . . .

Removal of IV   pulse 16   pull—

                    •

Use the Poisson equation to describe
the probability distribution
of random mutations in a cell that
affect ("hit") a particular gene ("target"):

                    •

Touch the eyelid closed with a damp finger—

                    •

$$P_x = \frac{h^x \, e^{-h}}{x!}$$

                    •

Playing Clue   counting her bean jars pinging—

                    •

Rick's oaks died because they were all alike—
chestnut blight, emerald ash bore, oak wilt,
Dutch elm disease, laminated root rot,
aspen canker, bacterial wetwood—

                    •

The amount of fossil fuel required to cremate the North American
crop of bodies each year has been estimated to equal what an
automobile would use in more than eighty round trips to the moon.

                    •

Good night *moon* good night *ACE inhibitors*
good night (to misquote myself) *farmhouse, fields*

good night *noises everywhere* good night *comb*—

    •

One raven :: rearranging the meat—

    •

I will do it—

—row on thousands of rows of yard-sale goods,
acres-to-let signs, falling-down silos.
The genetic modifications are
to enhance growth and durability.
The genetic modifications are
to enhance growth in corporate profits.
Here is your examination: Choose one.

Kernel :: cell :: syllable   I am her son

•

Use the swab   *sign here*   She is my mother

•

[*Hamartia*]

Poisons
the soil
to kill
the worm
that eats
the corn
that grows
in soil

•

So what's the *subject*?   water for the gums—

Meanwhile the haze air   and that calling pair

of doves farther apart   than you might suppose

flutes made of grasses   lower than her breath

until a jay cuts through   that scold that nag

on a moment's light   washing of breeze

yet all the trees blow   and simmer   above

which now many miles   across the village

the hot rods start up   guttural again

on a lit dust track   to see in a few

minutes which one may   cross over where

they all set off once   together   not now—

Untie the knots
        of your knuckles
    forgetting—

A short ride in   the van, then
the eight of us   there in the heat,

white shirtsleeves   sticking, the women's
gloves off—   fanning our faces.

The workers   had set up
a big blue tent   to help us at grave-

side tolerate   the sun, which
was brutal all   afternoon, as if

stationed above us,   though it
edged limb to   limb through

two huge covering   elms—the long
processional of   neighbors, friends,

the town's elderly,   her beauty shop
familiars, her   club's notables . . .

The world is full   of prayers
arrived at from   afterwards,

he said. Look   up   through the trees—
the leaves,   curled there as

in self-control   or quietly hurting
or now open, flat-   palmed, many-

fine-veined,   and whether from
heat or sadness,   waving—

Tell me your relation to pain, and I will tell you who you are!

I am looking at trees
they may be one of the things I will miss
most from the earth

she is my ::   *cover her*   *when she sleeps*

Under English ivy

        the Bishop's weed

and its variegated

        soft sage blue-

and-teal each plant

        a labyrinthine mass

of roots so pulling

        up of one mandates

the pulling now of

        many, many-yards

long and under these

        the pachysandra

folded splayed but

        uncovered suddenly

to spring upright

        the lacelike tendril ferns

the hard starved-for-sun

        pale pathos of the

hostas the yard beneath

        my yard I find

as though beneath the

        mind another mind—

•

*But trees do not dwell only in the present. They remember the
past, and they anticipate the future. . . . How trees remember, I
do not know. I have not been able to find out.*

as under dogwoods ferns

as under mounds

of leaves and rank half

bales of straw a mass

of hanging baskets

trashed after our glad

seasons and shards of

terra cotta pots

soft shouldered from

weathering and under

all of this the reeking

leaves and mulch become

rich loam again

I wheel it all barrow

by barrow to feed

the acrid hardpan

where the hungry

hollies the shallow-

rooted lilies of the

valley try to grow

I trowel it in   I

feed the earth the earth—

from

Never-Ending Birds

Trillium

1.

The first year I found it I found it by
accident, working my machete
to make out of the woods a walking path.
Not quite creekside, but in the tree shadow
of the creek, *trilliaceae*, or birthroot,
wake-robin, or any kind of lily
whose petals might wake a robin into
wings, as this does, three-winged if not
creekside, but close, beneath a hedge apple—
itself not an apple. Its blossom is
like a lily, in this case *Trillium*
flexipes (for drooping), as I found
the next year, maroon under three leaves
and swinging there like a bell. The little
brown-red bell blossom was gone the next day.
And the next year: knocked or nosed down by deer.

2.

Picking the flower of trillium can
injure the plant seriously, says my
book. May die or take years to recover.
So I built barricades of small branches,
cages, crossbars, as soon as these new leaves
uncapped, to keep out the deer yet airy
enough to let in some sun, ephemeral
angel wing of blossoms, half as light in
the green long shadow of wild rye grasses.
And the shadowy maroon blossoms hung
for a week—more—browned, peeled, seeded, then dropped.
The next year the drought year. Yet I've found it

again this April, walking the path. Which
is not my path. Not anymore. The deer
have fled, as well, deeper away from us.
And us not us anymore. Obstinate blooms.

Posthumous Man

I hate the world.
I have come to the edge.

A neighbor's white
bean field in the snow fog.

Three weeks of it
shedding in the warmth

like smoke from fire
lines set against the trees

or the season's
cold boredom with itself.

Mud in the white
field. A hump of gray snow.

Nothing is there.
I hold the dog tight

on his leash. Gray
snow: gray coat, rising now

—scuffed like a bad
rug, scruff-eared—so we watch

nothing rise in
the white bean field and shake

off a night's sleep
and sniff, sniff, peer over

at us. Winter
wrens in a fluff. Rustle

of bramble. He
trots off at precisely

one hundred and
eighty degrees from where

we emerged from
the woods, into the woods . . .

The long married abide in privacy
longer and longer. That's one irony.
After hearing the coyote crying
a week, ten days, maybe more, late at night
through the glassy air, crying like a bird
his song among the billion stars, we saw him
sunning asleep in the neighbor's old field.

And he woke. And saw us. And, unafraid,
loped off. We rise each morning alone from
the shape of our bodies in flannel sheets,
burrow beside burrow, where we dream of
running, bleeding, food, feral sex, each
to his or her own outlandish nightlife.
We walk in the world, we sip our coffee

at a clean glass table, we love our child.
Then come to an edge, where the world
meets the soul, and the soul knows once more
what it holds, such capacity
to inflict harm or injury, easy
as snowfall and fog's long rise back.
It does, it does not, again and again.

I hate the world.
It batters too much the

wings of my self-
will. He's writing to Fanny

a few weeks cold
after the nightingale.

He hears it sing
in lone, full-throated ease.

And knows himself
grown spectre-thin. Even

in sweet incense,
full summer, his sadness is

a bell's bird-call
tolling him *back from thee*

to my sole self!
He'll sail himself, next year—

a man post-
poetry and posthumous,

too numb to feel
the sun over Naples,

to heal his
scavenger lungs. His hands are

white cold. His nails
are ridged, like a field.

He writes, to Brown,
were I in health it would

make me ill. And
means, of course, his heart's lack

—white trees,
                    white waves—.

Behind me, winter wind. It whips
the sycamores, whose leaves are large as sheets
of paper, brittle brown or blowing down.
It shakes the blanched-out trunks of beech.
Despite the cold it's humid, a warm
exhaust of fog and breathing of the mud.
Back down the path I cut one summer, down

the ridge and up the drumlin rise beside
the creek, you're reading. Or you're watching
out the window where I vanished with a dog.
I learned when I should leave. There's privacy
you crave, as I do. The irony thereof—.
My sheltie wants, growling at his leash, loose.
The coyote would kill him simply.

So we watch. Long snout. Bone-slender, his high
rear hips. He's a reel of fog unspooling
toward the far, half-shadowed rim of trees.
Uptick of grackles, more wrens—.
                                        He's loping.
Now he's running through the field toward the woods.
By the time he is halfway he is gone.

The Rumor

Come home.
The earth utters
    to the body, and so the body does
      —come home—at last.

Consider thus
the tufts and tail piece,
    hooves cleft from the legs, the legs
      what's left of them where

they dropped con-
centric beneath
    the beech. Consider the beech,
      the lovers' owne

tree, this one, yes,
hearts scored-in
    and someone's, and someone else's, initials
      so swollen

they're unreadable and
more-than-head-
    high-up the trunk.
    Up the trunk—where the body crawled.

Think of that.
A furious, rapt hunger.
    We thought it a rumor
    when the farmer

called the paper,
when deputies spotted
    something—
    "buff deer or maybe a Dane running

loose in the
corn"—in the feedlot,
     three nights running. Look.
     There is no doubt whatever.

So the body,
even the lover, comes
     down to the earth. But not,
     this time, at first.

The big cat dragged
the corpse up
     the tree—they
     will do that, that's how we know, cats being

climbers
with prey they've killed
     —up, by the bole, the big place,
     to the crotch of the tree, that's what

we call it.
And crouched; ate; shat;
     even slept. The claw marks
     proceed up the tree. The fleshy

dun bark, blood
stripped brown as
     fox coat or
     wet sandstone, blood ascending the tree's

evident body. Up
the lovers' tree.
     Then the body fell, at
     least in little pieces,

all around the trunk,
spattered, strewn—
    aureole of deer guts, bitten
    skin, bone. The rest went

on again,
in the body of the beast.
    And so—we hear—the lovers
    do this, too.

Horse Madness

1.

means fury; means heat.
    From *Hippomanes*,
in Ferry's rendering
of Virgil's third georgic:
is slick with froth; is blood-
lipped; is spring-wild.
I see it in your eyes.
The horse is meant,
    like us, for madness.
It must be held in halter

lest it rear or run.
    It must be *scanted of*
leafy foods come
spring, to make it lean,
make it less familiar.
These things Virgil knows.
Yet it may run or rear
or with alarm
    betray your presence,
despite your care.

The eyes go everywhere.
    The eyes are orbital, animal;
they reflect both worlds.
So *Jackanappes-*
on-horsebacke
—weed we hold
as common marigold—
wraps a sun inside
    its petal before
the sun starts down . . .

2.

Their eyes were my clock.
  Thus the oval eyes
of goats and sheep
turn rounder as the day
goes down. Turn round to see,
in thirst, in pain or panic,
what gallops near, whatever
holds itself away, grinding
  in the brooding dust.
What makes Virgil

so compelling, beyond
  the grace of verse, is
farmer knowledge:
thus the shepherd sings
he finds his likeness
in their eyes. His judgment
grows of patience, as
practice grows of prudence,
  as goats deserve
no less than sheep deserve . . .

3.

Means burning-in-the-
  marrow; means as-they-
rush-into-the-fire. Meaning
all of us. I look at you
and find—what? Mythology,
song. Thus slaughter begins,
among the bullocks,
when bees are lost
  and must be raised again.
The nose is stopped

(who devised an art
    like this?) and the body
beat until its innards fall.
Then—with marjoram—
a ferment. Then the offal
seeds with bees, and up
they may be gathered.
    Meaning madness
is its own mythology.

The horse begins
    to tremble. The body
shivers; nor whip, nor reins,
nor wide opposing river,
whose rising *can*
bring down mountains,
may hold one back. I see it
in your eyes. Means
    the face I see is not,
my love, my face.

Never-Ending Birds

That's us pointing to the clouds. Those are clouds
of birds, now we see, one whole cloud of birds.

There we are pointing out the car windows.
October. Gray-blue-white olio of birds.

Never-ending birds, you called the first time—
years we say it, the three of us, any

two of us, one of those just endearments.
Apt clarities. Kiss on the lips of hope.

I have another house. Now you have two.
That's us pointing with our delible whorls

into the faraway, the trueborn blue-
white unfeathering cloud of another year.

Another sheet of their never ending.
There's your mother wetting back your wild curl.

I'm your father. That's us three, pointing up.
Dear girl. They will not—it's we who do—end.

Bay

Heat shirrs the water
where it's spilled—*have to*
get him in
 just the right spot,

it's
quick, he'll go
heavy when his back hits
 the grass—trough like a silver sleeve

at the barn side.
Now my neighbor flicks (it's
thick as a Coke
 bottle) his hypo. Says

now and the colt
tips over,
forgets those slender knees.
 And now he swabs a spot—

have to hurry—clippers
the musky hide down
to the skin
 brown as a grocery sack and

ties his
hind leg, then the other.
It's my job to pull the risen one, spread
 up, woody mirage in the mud

across the pen,
rope behind my neck,
arm eagled out
 along the running guywire, colt's

hoof high in the air.
Now my friend's got his
vicious tool more
    like a sharp sickle or meat hook than a

surgical device,
but really
that's what it is, silver hook
    to slit

the tough skin and
tease out the testicles,
so he does, hand
    inside, snip snip, tossing the first small

red wad
for the dog—but *goddamn* is
what he says, ooze now, some flesh-
    bubble, and the anesthesia

already easing off—
close him up
before it's all leaked out—undevel-
    oped wall and herniating guts where the hand is still

half in, *can't do this* . . .
But the colt
is bobbing his neck, leg
    pulled harder along my neck rope, a little shit

running from his tail:
what I meant
to say is
    —it happens so fast—I grabbed his

neck, fingers in his mane
as he softened, first, to fall,
and that's
     when I thought of us, dancing

in the dining room,
hands in each other's
clothes and the woody bay-plant's
     saucer overfull, and one

leaf snapped—that's it, that scent—.

Too Many

my neighbors
say, when what they mean
    are deer—the foragers, the few at a time, fair

if little more
than rats, according to
    a farmer friend nearby, whose corn means plenty.

They nip the peaches,
and one bite ruins;
    hazard every road with their running-

into-headlights-
not-away; a
    menace; plague; something should be done.

   Or here in town,
where I've
    found a kind of afterlife—the townies hate

the damage to their varie-
gated hostas,
    shadeside ferns—what they do inside white bunkers of

the county's one good
course is "criminal,"
    deep scuffs through the sand—that's one thing—but

lush piles of polished-
olive-droppings, hoof-
    ruts in the chemically- and color-enriched greens . . .

Yet here's
one more, curled
        like a tan seashell not a foot from my blade, just-

come-to-the-
world fawn, speckled,
        wet as a trout, which I didn't see, hacking back

brush beneath my tulip
poplar—it's not afraid,
        mews like a kitten, can't walk: there are so many, too

many of us,
the world keeps saying,
        and the world keeps making—this makes no sense—
                more.

from

Midwest Eclogue

Monarchs Landing and Flying

If they have come for the butterflies then
bless their breaking hearts, but the young pair is
looking nowhere except each other's eyes.
He seems like he could carry them both
over the street on great wings of grief tucked
under his coat, while all around them float,
like wisps of ash or the delicate
prism sunlight flashing off the city glass,
the orange-yellow-black-wing-flecked monarchs.
Migrant, they're more than two dozen today,
more long-lived than the species who keep
to the localized gardens—they're barely
a gram apiece, landing, holding still for
the common milkweed that feeds their larvae,
or balanced on bridges of plume grass stalks
and bottlebrush, wings fanning, closing, calmed
by the long searchlight stems of hollyhock.
If they have come for the butterflies then
why is she weeping when he lifts her chin?
He looks like he's holding his breath back—
or is he trying to shed tears, too? Are
any left? He's got his other hand
raised, waving, and almost before it stops
the taxi's doors flare on both sides open.
Nothing's stirring in the garden, not us,
not the thinnest breeze among the flowers,
yet by the time we look again they've flown.

Hyper-

Then a stillness descended the blue hills.
I say stillness. They were three deer, then four.
They crept down the old bean field, these four deer,
for fifteen minutes—more—as we watched them

in the field, in the soughing snow. That's how
slowly they moved in stillness, slender deer.
The fourth limped behind the other three,
we could see, even in the darkness, as it

dragged its right hindquarter where it was
hit or shot. Katie sat back on her heels.
The dog held in his prints, or Kate held him,
hardly breathing at first. Then we relaxed.

Blue night descended our neighbor's blown hills.
And the calm that comes with seeing something
beautiful but far from perfect descended—
absolute attention, a fixity.

I say absolute. It was stillness.

In the books we gathered, the first theory
holds that the condition's emergence is
most common at age eight, if less in girls
than boys, or more vividly seen in boys
whose fidgets, whose deficit attentions,
like little psycho-economic realms,
are prone to twitches-turned-to-virulence,
anxieties palpable in vocalized
explosions—though now we know in girls
it's only on the surface less severe,

which explains her months of bubbling tension,
her long blue drifts and snowy distractions.
I say distractions. Of course I mean how,
clinically, tyrosine hydroxylase
activity—the "rate limiting enzyme
in dopamine synthesis"—disrupts, burns,
then rewires her brain's chemical pathways.

Let me put it another way. After
twenty-four math problems, the twenty-fifth
still baffles her, pencil gnawed, eraser-
scuff-shadows like black veins on her homework.

It's not just the theory of division
she no longer gets, it's her hot clothes, her
itchy ear, the ruby-throated hummingbird's
picture on the fridge, what's in the fridge, whose

socks these are, why, until I'm exhausted
and yell again. Until she's gone away
to her room, lights off, to sulk, read, cry, draw.
No longer trusting to memory, she

writes everything in her journal now, then
ties it with a broken strand of necklace.
Of her friends: *I am the funny one.* Mom:
She has red hair and freckles to. Under Dad:

I have his bad temper. I know. I looked.

In one sketch she finished, just before we
learned what was wrong—I mean, before we knew
what to call what was wrong, how to treat it,
how to treat *her*—she captured her favorite
cat with a skill that skips across my chest.

He's on a throw rug, asleep. The rug's fringe
ruffles just so. The measure of her love is
visible in each delicate stroke, from
his fetal repose, ears down, eyes sealed
softly, paws curled inward, to the tiger lines
of his coat deepened by thick textures
where she's slightly rubbed away the contours
with her thumb to winter coat gray. He's soft,
he's purring, he's utterly relaxed asleep.
One day, before we learned what was wrong,
she taped it to a pillow on my bed.
Terry Is Tired she'd printed at the top.

How many ways do we measure things by
what they're not. I say things. Mostly her mind
is going too fast, yet the doctors give her,
I'm not kidding, amphetamines—

speed, we used to say, when we needed it—
Ritalin, which wears off hard and often,
Adderal, which lasts all day though her food's
untouched and sleep comes late. The irony

is the medicine slows her down. She pays
attention, understands things. The theory
is, AD/HD patients "aren't hyper-
aroused, they're underaroused," so they lurch

and hurtle forward, hungry for focus.
Another theory says the brain's two lobes
are missized. Their circuits "lose their balance."
One makes much of handedness—left—red hair,

allergies, wan skin, an Irish past . . .

We watched four deer in stillness walking there.
Stillness walking, like the young blue deer hurt
but beautiful. In her theory of
division, Katie's started drawing them—
her rendering's reduced them down to three.
She has carefully lined the cut bean rows
in contours like the dog's brushed coat. Snowflakes
dot the winter paper. Two small deer stand
alert on either side of the hurt one
leaning now to bite the season's dried-up stems.
Their ears are perched like hands, noses up, tails
tufted in a hundred tiny pencil lines.
She's been hunkered over her drawing pad,
humming, for an hour. So I watch. I say
watch. I ask why she's made the little hurt
one so big. Silly. He's not hurt that bad,
she says. She doesn't look up. That one's you.

The Spring Ephemerals

Here she comes with her face to be kissed. Here she comes
lugging two plastic sacks looped over her arms and stuffed

with fresh shoots. It's barely dawn. She's been out
for an hour already, digging up what she can save

before developers raze the day's lot sites and set woodpiles
ablaze. That's their plan for the ninety-plus acres.

She squats in the sun to show me wild phlox
in pink-running-to-blue, rue anemone, masses

of colt's foot, wild ginger, blood root and may-
apples, bracken and fiddlehead fern—ferns being not

spring ephemerals per se, but imperiled by road graders
come to shave the shaded slopes where they grow.

Once I held her in a snow cover of sheets. Wind beat
the world while we listened. Her back was a sail,

unfurling. She wanted me to touch stitches there,
little scabs, where doctors had sliced the sick cells

and cauterized her skin for safety's sake.
Now her hands are spotted by briars, bubbles of blood

daubed in brown. She's got burrs in her red hair.
Both sleeves are torn. She kneels as the sunlight

cuts through pine needles above us, casting a grid
like the plats the surveyors use. It's the irony

of every cell: that it divides to multiply.
This way the greedy have bought up the land

behind ours to parcel for resale at twenty-
fold what they paid weeks ago.

It's a race to outrun their gas cans and matches,
to line the path to our creek with transplants

of spice bush, yellow fawn lily, to set aside space
in the garden for the frail. She adjusts the map

she's drawn of the tumbling woods—where each
flower and fern come from, under what tree, beside

which ridge. *Dysfunctional junctional nevus*:
a name like a bad joke for the growth on her skin,

pigment too pale for much sunlight. *Drooping trillium*,
she says, handing me a cluster of roots, unfolding leaves—

rare around here. How delicate, a trillium,
whose oils are food for ants, whose sessile leaves are

palm-sized, tripartite. They spread a shadow over
each stem's fragile one bloom, white in most cases,

though this one's maroon. This makes it rarer.
It hangs like a red bell safe from the sun. It bends

like our necks bend, not in grief, not prayer,
as we work with our backs to the trees, as they burn.

Winged

If this were the sea and not snow, morning-
cold, Ohio, the slick black trees standing
for themselves along our ice creek, then
these birds might seem ready for the flight.
They've opened their massive wings, five,
six feet across, and hold them to the cold sun
as though cutting through salt winds unfettered.
This dries them. But how eerie they look,
like the stonework of graves, like gargoyles
dripping and grim in the precision of faith.
They have settled on just one tree. Sunlit,
they are black blooms, their heads wrinkled
as walnuts, each with a small smear of blood
for a face. If this were the sea. But it's not.
If she were alive and yesterday's procession
of black cars, flutter of flags, were something
other than what they were, like wisps of smoke
sent up from the steamer churning for home,
then we might know at least the gods await.
That the ash does cleanse. And the afterlife
shall yield us great wings for the body
to fly where the others, it seems, have gone.

Midwest Eclogue

We wade into a blackened pond to save
        the dying water.
        The water isn't dying
—we know, we know—it's the fish and frogs
        starving, pushed out
        by subsurface growth.

Still, that's how they put it to us,
        our new neighbors
        who've come
to watch us cope with our
        stagnant, weedy, quarter-acre
        runoff swamp.

They say let it go, by which they mean
        (this from Scott, cut
        like a side of beef,
six-pack belted like a holster to his pants)
        it's God's will, or nature's, and besides
        it's too much work,

to which his father John, bigger, bald
        scorch of a face, plops
        on our dock and says you
got that right. At first we tried sprinkling
        chemicals around
        the darkening perimeter—to wit,

copper sulfate penta-
        hydrate ($CuSO_4 \cdot 5H_2O$),
        used variously as
a micronized fungicide in pellets,
        a crystalline pesticide "noted
        for acute toxicity in bees,"

and here, a powdery "powerhouse" algaecide—
    or in other words (this
    from John), fancy sunblock
for the water. For weeks the bottom-
    black surface glowed
    eerily aquamarine,

yet all that died were two fat grass carp,
    lazy from the slime
    they ate, who floated up
like scaly logs to petrify. That's why
    I'm waist-deep
    where my neighbors watch,

rowing with a rake through
    a sludge of leaves,
    stirring algae
in a cooking pot. Each time I pull a gob
    of slime and glop, dark
    as organs, toward shore,

John yells out, encouraging, *that's* a good one,
    and I shove it on
    to rake up the bank
where we can haul it off sometime.
    Don't just sit there
    in the willow shade,

I ought to shout. Come on. Help us out.
    Or (this from Virgil via
    Corydon), why not at least
go about some needful task? But there's
    so much trouble
    in the world these days

I've been content to work in peace
  beside my life's
  surprising love, to keep
the cardinals throbbing in our close cattails
  and frogs at home
  in a splash of breathable water.

Each step stirs a slick
  of spreading ooze
  that follows
orbital in my wake, nebulae of oil
  and algae stars. And look,
  overhead the first real star

has answered back: There's darkness
  on the way. We drag another
  sloppy mass up the bank
and see its dimming possibilities—
  tadpoles and minnows,
  shiny as coins, egg-

clusters of sun perch, bluegill roe—
  throbbing in the grass,
  twisting to be loose, aglow
against the color of the coming night. And there go
  John and Scott, down
  on their knees in the grass,

untangling as many as they can to slip back
  to the black pond, before the sky
  turns black as well.
There's smoke you can see from the neighbors' chimney,
  and the shadows of the hills are
  lengthening as they fall.

The Blue

heron is gray, not blue, but great enough
against brown-tipped bowed cattails to be
well-named, is known for its stealth, shier
than a cloud, but won't fly or float away
when it's scared, stands there thinking maybe
it's invisible though it's not—tall, gray,
straight as a pole among the cloudy reeds.

Then it picks up one stem leg. This takes time.
And sets it down just beyond the other,
no splash, breath of a ripple, goes on
slowly across the silt, mud, algae-
throttled surface, through sedge grass,
to stand to its knees in water turning
grayer now that afternoon is evening.

Now that afternoon is evening
the gray heron turns blue, bluer than sky,
bluer than the mercury blue-black still pond.
So when did it snag the bullfrog
hanging, kicking, in its scissor beak?
To look so long means to miss the sudden.
It strides around like a sleek cat

from pond to bank and back, blue tall bird,
washing the frog, banging it against stones,
pecking almost as if it doesn't know
what to do now that it's caught such a thing.
How fast its beak must be to shoot out
like an arrow or that certain—as it's called—
slant of light. Blue light. Where did it go?

Late Pastoral

1.

At first only fog lifting off
the snow and snow
      sifting through it,
      then Pepper pointing to the last

pocket of night among
the densest pines,
      each life for an instant
      in calm regard of the other, and the deep breath

shuddered—the *whomff*—the stern
explosion meant
      not to startle but warn,
      so the big doe stood her ground, then

ran. Or not, being lame, she being
the solitary deer
      four times this week
      up close to the house with her three-

footed hobble, her track
with its triplet prints
      and unmistakable scuff
      where a back leg drags through the drifts.

There's nothing below
where the slender knee should be.
      Nonetheless,
      she has vanished, shadow among shadows

back to the woods, taking her tattered
rags of breath,
          a fluff of tail,
          the sheltie straining at his leash.

2.

And of that sound,
what can I tell you?—
          lingering deep
          as a bear's, drawn up from the gut, chest

broadened until her breath blows out
with great force, plosive
          at the nose.
          The sound's like the *swumpp* of snow sliding

off the eaves, inevitable action-at-
a-distance
          of gravity
          from spring's slow melt.

The ancients thought such behaviors were
rooted in the nature of things
           in themselves
          —arrows dying, a stone in the creek—whose counter-

weight they saw in a floating feather
as levity,
          as in wood, wind, or
          the spirit of the doomed and beloved arising.

My hunter neighbor says
the sound is a feature
          of wilder
          deer. Not those accustomed to our houses and smells,

our noise, who sift softly among
trash cans and orchards
   and flee
    before we know they're among us.

3.

It's the acorns she comes for,
there being nothing to eat
   in the woods,
    the woods being iced over, snow-solid, for weeks.

I have found
only
   the gnawed and spat
    splatter of hedge apples, that's how desperate

they are, driven toward us
by nothing to forage,
   by vanishing trees
    and razed fields, by exurbs, by white-

flight and our insatiate hunger for size
and space and tax
   advantages. She grubs down,
    she snuffles under oaks, blowing back snow

to chew the hard nubbin acorns
though they're frozen,
   squirrel-hollowed,
    and sparse. I have watched her

from my dark window.
I have felt the gravity of her days.
   Little
    remains. We have

a new dog, did I tell you?
He bears
    his lineage well—from those pastoral herders
    of ancient highlands, who

accompanied us, who helped us,
and who from a distance seem almost
        —wouldn't you say it's still so?—
    to float.

from

Changeable Thunder

Benton's Clouds

The background is clouds and clouds above those
the color of an exhaustion, whether
of field hands stacking sheaves, or the coiling,
columnar exhaust of a coal engine.

It is eighteen seventy in nineteen
twenty-seven in nineteen ninety-eight.
The colors of his clouds express each new
or brooding effluence felt elsewhere as

progress, no matter which foreground story,
no matter the gandy dancer contoured
as corn field, no matter Persephone
naked as herself, as a sinew of

rock ledge or oak root yet pornographic
under the modern elder leering down.
The background is everywhere telling.
In the present moment, in the real air,

what we saw above the lake was an art—
gulls and then no gulls, swirl of vacation
debris twirling in funnels from the pier
though the wind rushed in wilder off the surge,

clouds, then not clouds but a green-gray progress
of violences in the lowing air, waves
like a bad blow under water. We stood
at the pier railing and watched it come on.

It is too late to behold the future,
if by future what we mean is the passed-
over detail in the painting which tells
where the scene is destined to lead—Benton's

brilliance, beside the roiling billowy
cloud banks blackened as battlefield debris,
beside the shapely physique of nature
on the move, its machinery of change,

is history in an instant. How else
infuse his Reconstruction pastorals,
his dreamy midwifes, sod farmers, dancing
hay bales wrapped in billows of sallow light,

with an agony befitting the some-
time expatriate Modernist Wobbly
harmonica player he was. Who else
could execute such a beautiful storm,

whipped white, first a color on the water
like a wing or natural improvement.
When the Coast Guard boat swept by us waving,
it was already too late and too close.

The storm took down the big tree in seconds.
Though we were running, swirl of muscle, bales
and billows of fear like the wind breaking
over each swell with the force of a hand,

though we cleared the first breakwall and elm grove,
it was only accident the baby's
carriage was not crushed by the linden bough
sheared off, clean as a stick. We were standing

in the grinding rain, too soon still for tears.
It was too soon to tell what damages
there would be, though we knew, as in his art,
as though before the last skier had tipped

into the lake, there was peril ahead.
We could see it all in an instant's clear
likeness, where the future is not coming
but is already part of the story.

Pulp Fiction

You want more? You want some more of this *shit?*
so he puts his weight to his elbow jammed
under the jaw of the other one pinned
there, panicked, panting, his back to the bricks.
The others are loud and jeering and stand
in a jackal circle a spitting length
away. The cold air is full of bird song.

The sex—sheer sugar—of the flowering trees
turns to powder against the skin, and cakes
the sidewalks pale green, and packs the curbs.
Far away a powerful siren cries.
Someone is about to get his ass kicked.
But now the cruel gang spots someone—okay,
it's me—who is writing this whole scene down.

It's so easy to surpass the limits
of the powers of description. *What are*
you *looking at?* There are yellow flowers
sprouting from the downspout above their heads.
The powers of discursion are no less
feeble, frail as the least petal. *Stop it!*
They don't stop it. The one in trouble is

starting to weep, and the others to laugh,
as the one with the elbow suddenly
slips a white-handled knife from his pocket.
(Is this the big city? Are there dime bags
dropping from the claws of carrion birds?
Have his bad colors taunted the wrong turf?)
No. No. No. This is just my little town,

and the hostile gang is as easily
eight years old as twenty, out of grade school
since three o'clock. I'm sorry for my mind,
but the spring has spread a violent seed
and it has taken root in this poem,
as in my heart, in the children beating
each other to a pulp in your city

as well as mine. Is it less barbarous
to turn now toward the beautiful? Once
there was a hillside of white, wild lilies.
The mayapples were spilling there. A first
green froth of spring ferns spread under the pines—
so the pastoral, unperturbed lilies
stand around our absence in the sunlight.

What have we done to deserve the pollen,
the plant persistence, of our natures? You
want more? The boys beat the daylights out of
the poor boy and I do nothing to help.
And the flowers are fiction—descriptive,
discursive—designed to suggest my mind
in peace or shame. So are the boys, if

the truth be told. So are the sexual trees.
The knife, you understand, is real. The knife is mine.

Trees beside Water

1.

                    Stag-
headed elders, the book
calls them, trash trees.

The protrusive is
what the eye draws to—
not the canopy of leaves

but their stripped
limbs sticking through.
This makes the elders

seem stunted beside
the pond sycamores.
To waken, not having

slept, is to find
oneself on the other
side of the shore.

2.

For months I lie down
in a fever. When I
look out, as over

landscape, when my night
fills with brambles—
the rope, the blood-braid

of the briar rose
spreading a dark shore—
I feel the veins of

my body looping
with poison, ripened
with lymph. I lie down

in the night, and my
tree swells within me,
jagged, wild, thorned.

3.

And so the sky fills—
so my limbs shudder,
as on a breeze, when

something with claws lifts
and lands again down
the length of the shore.

What commerce is a
breeze, which our elders
called "an ether, so

fine a liquid one
might sail there," as clouds
of stars rinse from the

sky like waste, water,
fever of leaves on
an eddy of sweat.

4.

Sometimes I cry out
and no one hears me.
Sometimes, even now,

I can't tell the trees
from a force in the
wind or the words

in a book. And my
night goes on wildly,
virus, cell, and cloud.

Sleep is a book
the elders have written.
New limbs break through

mantles of old leaves.
I am a few leaves,
pressed in the book.

After Rain

1.

You have to turn your back to the animals.
      In theory it's better for them than shoes.
You have to hold them one leg at a time
      pinched with your legs to pick clean beneath each
hoof the sawdust, straw, mud-pack, pebbles, dung.
      The old ones stand patient while the young may
stomp the hard barn floor to tell you to quit
      or nod their long necks or quiver or huff.

2.

Rain has turned them skittish, the rain-flung leaves,
      whatever flies or crawls from a cold tree.
The scrape of your moon-crescent blade, as you
      carve each hoof hard as plastic or soft wood
down to the white heart, makes them want to grow
      wings, makes them want to fly or die or run.
You have to talk them down. Easy, you say
      in your own wind, soothing, easy now, whoa.

3.

But it's the long, continuous sighing
      breath of the file that stills them, for they know
you are through. You round the last edges down
      and smooth the hard breaks, as one by one they trot
through the tack room door, muscle, mane, shadow,
      turning their backs to you. Now the sun is out.
Barn swallows brighten the loft. You watch them
      break into flight, hoofprints filling with rain.

The City of God

Now we knelt beside
the ruined waters
as our first blood,
our bulb-before-bloom,
unfurled too early

in slender petals.
Now we were empty.
Now we walked for months
on softer shoes and
spoke, not quite with grief.

This morning four deer
come up to the yard
to stand, to be stunned,
at the woods' edge
on their hoof-tips. Their

ears twist like tuners,
but they stay for minutes,
minutes more, while
we are shadows behind
windows watching them

nip at the pine bark,
nibble some brown tips
of hydrangea. It's
been a mean, dry winter.
The last time I prayed—

prayed with any thought
of reply, any
hope of audience—

I sat in a church
and the city smell

of lilac, fumes from
the bus line, filled me.
The joys of the body
are not the sins
of the soul.

       Who knows
how many have come
to be with us? We
knelt, not as in prayer,
beside the toilet

and watched the first one
leave us utterly—.
They were deer. Now they
are fog.
       Now the wind

pulls back through the trees.
We know it will
be this way always
—whatever fades—
and the dreadful wake.

Unconditional Election

We have decided now to kill the doves
—November the third, nineteen ninety-nine—
who gather in great numbers in the fields
of Ohio, vast and diminishing,

whose call is gray and cream, wing-on-the-wind.
I lean from the deck to hear their mourning
cry, like the coo of a human union.
They persevere as song in the last days.

Or is it the wind I hear this morning,
crossing the great, cold lake, the hundred dry
miles of fields cut down to stubble and rust?
The rain gauge, hollow as a finger bone,

lifts to survey the stiffening breeze.
The boards of our deck are a plank bridge
hanging over nothing, the season's abyss.
When we decided not to have the child,

how could we know the judgment would carry
so far?—each breath, each day, another
renewal of our *no*. A few frail leaves
hurry now dryly in waves at my feet.

The doves have no natural predator,
so we will be their fate. We will prowl
the brown fields, taking aim at the wind,
or huddle inside in the lengthening dark.

It no longer matters who is right. Their cry
comes from both sides of the window at once.

Ohio Fields after Rain

The slow humped backs of ice ceased
to shadow the savannahs of Ohio millennia
ago, right where we've sailed to a stop.
The shaken woman leaves open her car door
and familiar as relatives we touch hands
in the middle of the wet, black road.
To the north new corn enriches by the hour.

South of us—really, just over a fence—
heavy boulders rolled thousands of miles
quit the migration and grew down,
huddled, cropped, scarred by the journey.
"I couldn't," she says, "stop skidding,"
and I know what she means, having
felt the weight of my car planing a scant

millimeter over the highway glaze. Calmly
she slid to one shoulder, I to the other,
and the earth spun onward without us.
What a place we have come to, scooped
hollow of hillsides, cut valleys, drumlins
and plains. And where the rain settles,
the gray beasts growing tame on the shore.

from

The Truth about
Small Towns

Still-Hildreth Sanitorium, 1936

When she wasn't on rounds, she was counting
the silver and bedpans, the pills in white cups,
heads in their beds, or she was scrubbing down

walls streaked with feces and food on a white-
wash of hours past midnight and morning, down
corridors quickened with shadows, with screaming,

the laminate of cheap disinfectant . . .
what madness to seal them together, infirm
and insane, whom the state had deemed mad.

The first time I saw them strapped in those beds,
caked with sores, some of them crying
or coughing up coal, some held in place

with cast-iron weights . . . I would waken again.
Her hands fluttered blue by my digital clock,
and I lay shaking, exhausted, soaked cold

in soiled bedclothes or draft. I choked on my pulse.
I ached from the weight of her stair-step quilt.
Each night was a door slipping open in the dark.

Imagine, a white suit for gimlets at noon.
This was my Hollywood star, come to be lost
among dirt farmers and tubercular poor.

He'd been forgotten when the talkies took hold.
He saw toads in webs drooping over his bed.
O noiseless, patient, *his voice would quake.*

He took to sawing his cuticles with butter knives
down to the bone and raw blood in the dark.
Then, he would lie back and wait for more drug.

And this was my illness, constant, insomnolent,
a burning of nerve hairs just under the eyelids,
corneal, limbic, under the skin, arterial,

osteal, scrotal, until each node of the four hundred
was a pinpoint of lymphatic fire and anguish
as she rocked beside me in the family dark.

In another year she would unspool fabrics
and match threads at Penney's, handling finery
among friends just a few blocks from the mansion-

turned-sickhouse. She would sing through the war
a nickel back   a greenback   a sawbuck   a penny
and, forty years later, die with only her daughter,

my mother, to hold her, who washed her face,
who changed her bedgowns and suffers to this day
over the dementia of the old woman weeping

mama, mama, curled like cut hair from the pain
of her own cells birthing in splinters of glass.
What madness to be driven so deep into self . . .

I would waken and find her there, waiting
with me through the bad nights when my heart
trembled clear through my skin, when my fat gut

shivered and wouldn't stop, when my liver swelled,
when piss burned through me like rope against rock.
She never knew it was me, my mother still says.

Yet what did I know in the chronic room where I died
each night and didn't die, where the evening news
and simple sitcoms set me weeping and broken?

I never got used to it. I think of them often,
down on my knees in the dark, cleaning up blood
or trying to feed them—who lost eight children to the Flu,

who murdered her sisters, who was broken in two
by a rogue tractor, who cast off his name . . .
Sometimes there was nothing the doctor could do.

What more can we know in our madness than this?
Someone slipped through my door to be there
—though I knew she was a decade gone—

whispering stories and cooling my forehead,
and all I could do in the heritable darkness was
lift like a good child my face to be kissed.

Yellow Lilies and Cypress Swamp

1.

So green against the standing water they're
nearly black, the sudden, wild lily stalks
cup their flames like candlesticks beyond which,
as though it bears no end, the cypress swamp
continues into steam and smoke. How
lilies grow here is anybody's guess—
an errant seed buried in some bird's wing.
Or they caught a hard spring blow, floating down.
They bloom amber in landscape hazed dull green,
darkly cool, yet dangerous enough we
must watch our step or fall upon the strange,
hard cypress knees bunched around each trunk.

And how the cypresses reach through shallow
pools for sturdiness, thickened at the base,
stretched like softened sinew. They span upwards
of seventy feet, delicate, high, arched
canopy of leaves, gauze-white in the light.
Above water their short knees go rough, dry.
Below they're veined, yellow-red, like agates
broken open or the small, torn tissues
of a body turned stone by cold neglect.
They shine in a black, clean foot of water—
mosses cling to them. Wild lilies burning
in a cypress swamp. We wish to hold them.

2.

High, lighted altar. Pews of fine-planed board.
And mourners filing past the burnished, closed
casket to kiss his photograph, to touch
the bright brass fittings, say their goodbyes now
that it's too late. When the preacher stands
to lead us all in song, we recall beauty
is most likely in these solemn places.
Not the song, too pious and commanding,
not the stained-glass lighting or white candles
thawing onto hand-rubbed ebony, not
the few friends torn apart, here to heal,
but like a sudden slash of blood in wind one
redwing blackbird flashing past a clear pane
under which spreads a fist of lilies in a vase—
like landscape cupped, held, kept. One gorgeous flame.

Holiday Bunting

He has handled the new piece like a stone,
has rubbed it, has worried the wood-work, he
has nicked with his nail the softening flesh,

and hours now in the hands of the whittler
the cube of white ash has taken on wings,
evidence of a slight, blunted beak, whorls

in the wood grain where feathers will follow,
trimmed, sanded, blued into detail, and dried.
It is greasy with the whittler's palm oils.

From the front porch it is Saturday, noon,
and white-hot with sunlight. July the 4th.
He has worked through the parade, the speeches,

the blue-smoking floats and fiddlers' show,
the town done up in flags, whipping like wheat,
the route roped off red-ragged in front of his house.

In flight the small bird is likely to blur,
quick to the air, blue wind, lost in a crowd.
But who holds it with his hands has captured

wild by a wing. Who carves the knuckled claw-
feet cut out of splinters, out of ash bark,
can stand up for himself for as long as

he wishes and bourbon to kill the close heat.
He makes a nest of shavings when he stands,
stretches, settles back down in his good chair.

And when the bird is finished, no more tail
feathers to sharpen, touch up with edging,
he will hand it around to the children

then release it to the night's keeping next
to the knife, whetted, washed, on the porch rail—
and all gone by morning, banner, noise, bird.

The Truth about Small Towns

1. *The Truth about Small Towns*

It never stops raining. The water tower's tarnished
as cutlery left damp in the widower's hutch.

If you walk slow (but don't stop), you're not from nearby.
All you can eat for a buck at the diner is

cream gravy on sourdough, blood sausage, and coffee.
Never lie. The preacher before this one dropped bombs

in the war and walked with a limp at parade time.
Until it burned, the old depot was a disco.

A café. A card shoppe. A parts place for combines.
Randy + Rhonda shows up each spring on the bridge.

If you walk fast you did it. Nothing's more lonesome
than money. (Who says shoppe?) It never rains.

2. *Graveyard*

Heat in the short field and dust scuffed up, glare
off the guard-tower glass where the three pickets
lean on their guns. The score is one to one.
Everybody's nervous but the inmates,
who joke around—they jostle, they hassle
the team of boys in trouble and their dads.
It's all in sport. The warden is the ump.
The flat bleachers are dotted with guards; no
one can recall the last time they got one
over the wall. The cons play hard, then lose.
And the warden springs for drinks all around—
something he calls *graveyard*, which is five kinds

of soda pop poured over ice into
each one's cup, until the cup overflows.

3. *Council Meeting*

The latest uproar: to allow Wendy's
to build another fast-food burger shack
on two acres of wetlands near Raccoon Creek,
or to permit the conservationist

well-to-do citizenry to keep their green
space and thus assure long, unsullied views
from their redwood decks, picture windows,
and backyards chemically rich as golf greens.

The paper's rife with spats, accusations,
pieties both ways. Wendy's promises
flowers, jobs. The citizens want this, too,
but want it five miles away where people

don't care about egrets, willows, good views.
Oh, it's going to be a long night: call
out for pizza, somebody brew some tea.
Then we'll all stand up for what we believe.

4. *Charming*

The remnant industry of a dying town's itself.
Faux charm, flaked paint, innuendo in a nasal twang.
Now the hardware store's got how-to kits to make
mushrooms out of plywood for the yard,

and the corner grocery's specialty this week
is mango chutney, good with rabbit, duck, or spread
for breakfast on a whole-wheat bagel fresh
each morning at the small patisserie across

the way from the red hotel. Which reminds me.
Legend has it that the five chipped divots
in the hotel wall—local lime and mortar—
are what remains of the town's last bad man.

His fiery death's renowned, but don't look now.
Someone with a camera's drawing down on you.

Tract

I will let the Republic alone until
the Republic comes to me.
Emerson

The political
trees are preparing

      leaves for the bonfire.

Scraped up with chokers
of chains, tractored to

      piles, their limbs, trunks, root-

work, earthworks will be
kindling, will come clean.

      Someone has seen.

The dogwood is dull
fog under oaks where

      webbings of small flags

and surveyors' stakes
crosshatch the spring hills.

      Soon the deer prints will

melt from the old runs
and all the slender

      streams glow red with silt.

Goodbye, farmhouse, fields.
Someone is whispering

      our futures into

the wind. Do you hear?
Hardhats stand roadside,

        pointing their car phones.

The meaningful trees
lie down, and they burn.

The Affair

1.

Then the long fencerow, that years ago had
heaved and buckled, took on a copper shine
in the sunset, the dew. A garlic haze
of cut pastures simmered fields away.

2.

They were flushed from sex—they were
traced with that other body, just parted.
They stood in the length of first fall waiting.
And their skin, that had been so willing,

3.

delible as ash to a trembling fingertip,
became its own again. One star, three.
Nothing good was going to happen. Night winds
lifted themselves out of wheat rows and shook

4.

off what had been done. So they turned
elsewhere. Her fingers gathered up her collar
softly in a bunch, and she put on a scarf.
It was not even cold. It was only cool.

Treatise on Touch

Whom to believe? This is our central task.
My love lies pierced in the throat by needles.
She holds still as a branch on the white cot.
It is a matter of training, of touch,

as the doctor probes the nerve ganglia
in the base of her neck. He pushes blind
with the tip of a needle to deaden
each nerve to her hurt hands without numbing

her eyes, her auditor channels, her heart,
or any other system wrapped a thin
thread away against the ladder of spine.
The worried nurse keeps talking aerobics

as she cocks her syringe of medicine—
when he whispers *aspirate*, quickly she
draws it into a clear tube like good air.
Inject and she presses, she shoots it in.

To the eye the grounds are custodial,
every shrub, rose, cluster of trees clipped
or shorn in devoted form, so children
see discipline as an order of care.

The pathway through the green, medieval yards
is the same, to church or to class, and lined
like cathedral rooftops with witnesses,
gargoyles in stoneworks, stations of the cross,

the melancholy watchers of the faith,
and the Sisters of Divine Providence
laid to rest in the nunnery graveyard
only steps off the path. To visit them

daily is a march the parochial
children dread. And when she brings me to see,
two decades since, I feel the remnant fear
in the way she holds herself, and anger,

the way the woman I love is a child
again watched by the watchers from above.
It is a game to kiss the air, whisper's-
breath over the lips, though the nuns waiting

whose sister lies still in her coffin think
the children will learn to love or fear their
own lives better, blessing the mouth of the
dead. Whom to believe? To the touch the grounds

are fertile, fruitful with pain, the needling
undergrowth, dense pollen brushed at the nose,
the figure of the martyr hung and pierced,
a hand struck in punishment from pure air . . .

Divine I am inside and out, and I
make holy whatever I touch or am
touched from . . . To touch my person to some one
else's is about as much as I can stand.

Now the nurse holds her hand steady to clear
the path the medicine takes through the tube.
They don't really know what is wrong. The weeks
have brought only pain, how the slightest touch

burns from the fingertips upward, wrists, fore-
arms, elbows, until even the muscle
mass, the tissue, atrophies. She cannot
hold a spoon or brush our child's hair to sleep.

She cannot hold her body still to sleep.
A doctor tells her, use them or they'll fail—
another thinks it best to wait and gives
her medicine though it makes her bleed,

as if miscarrying, pregnant from a
lover's touch she only dreamed she may have
known. Whom to believe? *The rays that come from*
heavenly worlds will separate between

him and what he touched.—The doctors don't agree.
There I feel that nothing can befall me
in life,—no disgrace, no calamity
(leaving me my eyes), which nature cannot

repair. Therefore,
                 I believe my love, who
lies still as a stone below her good nurse.
I believe the children walking the path,
watching the bees, and the bells which call them

to music or mass, immaculate song.
I believe this pain, which makes us all sing—
the song like a finger pointing down, damned,
and the eyes of the faithful gazing back.

from

After the Reunion

Snow Figure

1.

A humble night. Hush after hush. Are you listening?
That's what the snow says, crossing the ice.

And the blue creek out back—where my love and I came
early one morning to remember nothing but blue

and the muffled joy of a far night's nothingness—
the blue creek, teasing, wild beneath its ice,

says hush. Snow whiffs around on its glassine surface.
Why did we wish so hard to walk where it deepens?

Why did we want to hold hands here?
My love and I came to learn how to love

the little that skates on the surface,
the nothing that flies, fast and fatal, beneath.

2.

I have put in a poem what has fallen from my life
and what I would change. Are you here?

We left a slender pathway of tracks. It led nowhere,
if not to our bodies, and filled in our emptiness.

What I want most to say is what I never told her.
Don't trust me. Trust me. How could I lie?

3.

A figure of speech is where desire forces a crisis, a crossing—
one world and its weather suddenly brilliant with meaning.

My love and I came out early one morning to forget
the humble one night when the snow fell over us

and we filled each other's body with our own.
So the old snow burns crystal in the sun. So the ice

slipping the creek's edges keeps teasing to be tried—
Trust me, it brags, black, thrilling, or empty.

Why do we wish so hard to listen to what isn't here?
Here, the snow says, as if in response. My love was here.

Along the Storm Front

I didn't tell you. After the killing sun
had finally started to cool back out

of the bricks, heat lightning or a far
searchlight broke the clouds scudding the low sky.

I had gone out to the wild, split hickory
to find some comfort. Its bark was peeled back,

bones sticking through. All the earlier fierce
rain rose as steam, coating the leaves a little,

hanging in the wet heat; terrible wind
had ripped the hickory.

                        And then you were
beside me, swirl of your hair, your shocking

damp hand sliding along my arm, the quick,
filling desire to hold to you, the way

on the most dangerous summer days when
choking haze turns suddenly wild with wind,

dust driven up, sun and tornado can
be only minutes apart. There is no

explanation. Only the usual calm,
then the plane going down in the storm.

Red Shift

Only here, through the clear lens of language
and under

        the sparkling sky of a new
moon's night in a cold month, here

only
    —I have walked this far without you—

where the calm chill fractures each isolate
body like a glass,

        an emptying fear,
I have come, and stand, myself, abstract

as a star.
      All around, in the true deep

distances, the trillion trillion trillion
lovely others sail outward,

         each toward its
own blank end—shattered cells in a burst heart,

word waving
      goodbye—accelerating

in exact proportion to this moment,
darkening away

      down the visible
spectrum while I wait, here always, without you,

at the center of the extending,
                              memorial grief.

Faith

It was midday before we noticed it was morning.
The boy cousins brought us a tray—soup and cheese,
warm soda, and a soft cloth and candy for her fever.
They wouldn't come in, the tray weighing between them.
They stood like woodwork inside the door frame.

By afternoon the old procession—silence at the lip
of a dozen night travelers tired and grieving, one
by one, or pairs floating to the bed and back
with a touching of hands like humming,
and the one we gathered for slipping farther

for all the good we could do. She lay in her shadow.
She looked to no one. Her daylilies bobbed wide
open out in the wild, blue sun and the same bee
kept nosing her window to reach them.
Dusk: even the boys were back watching it try.

Murder

1.

Language must suffice.

Years ago,
         under a sweet June sky
stung with stars and swept back by black leaves
barely rustling,

a beautiful woman nearly killed me.

Listen,
she said,
and turned
her lovely face to the stars, the wild sky . . .

2.

No.

No: years ago,

         under a sweet, June sky
strung with stars and swept back by black leaves
barely rustling,

under this sky
broad, bright, all rung around

with rustling elders—or intoxicating willows,
or oaks, I forget—
         under this sky,

a beautiful woman killed me, nearly.

I say beautiful. You had to see her.

Listen,
she said,

and turned a lovely shell of her ear
to the swirl of stars
and the moon
                    smudged as a wingtip in one tree, not far.

3.

Yes: she scraped my back bloody against a rough trunk.
Yes: she flung back her lovely face
and her hair, holding me down,

and the tree shook slowly, as in a mild, persistent laugh
or wind,

                and the moon high in that black tree
shook to and fro . . .

there were millions of stars
up where she stared past us,
and one moon, I think.

4.

Excuse me.

My friend, who loves poetry truly, says too much
nature taints my work.

Yes. Yes. Yes.
Too many birds, stars—
                              too much rain,
                              too much grass—
so many wild, bowing limbs
howling or groaning into the nature night . . .

and he might be right. Even here.

That is, if *tree* were a tree.
That is, if *star* or *moon* or even *beautiful woman*
craning the shell of her ear
were what they were.

They are, I think, not.

No: and a poem about nature contains anything but.

5.

When they descended to us, they were a *cloud of stars*
sweeping *lightly.* They sang to us urgently
about our lives,

they touched us
with a *hundred thousand hair-soft, small legs—*

and held down by such hungers, we let them cover us,
this *beautiful woman,* this *me,*

who couldn't move,
who were *stung*—do you hear?—
were stung again, were covered that quickly, crying
to each other
                    to *fly away!*

6.

      . . . I just can't erase
the exquisite, weeping language
of the wasps, nor her face in starlight
and so tranquil under that false, papery, bobbing
      moon
just minutes before,
saying listen,

listen,

nor then the weight
of her whole natural body

                        pinning down mine
until we both cried out for fear, and pain,
and still couldn't move.

7.

Language must suffice.
First, it doesn't. Then, of course,

it does. *Listen, listen.*

What do you hear? This nearly killed me.
I'll never know
why she didn't just whisper *Here they come*, warn *Move!*
cry *They'll kill us!*
Yes: *I will save you . . .*
Yes: *I love you too much to watch you suffer!*
But it's all I recall, or now need.

And, anyway, I loved her, she was so beautiful.
And that is what I have had to say
before it's too late,

                                before they have killed me,
before they have killed you, too,

or before we have all become something else entirely,

which is to say
before we are
only language.

Mercy

Small flames afloat in blue duskfall, beneath trees
anonymous and hooded, the solemn tress—by ones
and twos and threes we go down to the water's level edge
with our candles cupped and melted into little pie-tins
to set our newest loss free. Everyone is here.

Everyone is wholly quiet in the river's hush and appropriate dark.
The tenuous fires slip from our palms and seem to settle
in the stilling water, but then float, ever so slowly,
in a loose string like a necklace's pearls spilled,
down the river barely as wide as a dusty road.

No one is singing, and no one leaves—we stand back
beneath the grieving trees on both banks, bowed but watching,
as our tiny boats pass like a long history of moons
reflected, or like notes in an elder's hymn, or like us,
death after death, around the far, awakening bend.

After the Reunion

To finish by picking up pieces of cake and small clutter
from the sunporch floor, to finish by cleaning up.

We couldn't tell them—not the host of relatives
happy to be on each other's hands again,

                                        each other's nerves.
The lilac hedge let go its whole bushel of odors

and our acre's birds kept the trees stitched
with their art. Everyone agreed.

Someone's boss is somebody's neighbor.
Who looks like whom in the crisp old albums?

—What kind of linen, what brand of seed, what
do you do when things get bad?

                                There is nothing
that does not connect and so sustain.

Now I want us to keep loving each other, too.
The strength it takes is their patience—

a stretching of legs, waiting long.
Who knows what sadnesses they have endured?

Who knows which ones we have caused?
Let's open the door and let the bluejays and sparrows

attend our repair. Let's take the whole day.
Let's keep forever the napkin our last waving aunt

pressed her kiss into—delicate red, already
powdered, doomed as a rose.

from
Sweet Home,
Saturday Night
and Haunts

November: The End of Myth

We parked beneath that poor, bending tree.
It was our mistake, all along.
We curled in our friends' mild cabin
cupping the mulled wine, leaning

to taste pears touched
in cinnamon, swaying there content
while the split wood wept and whiled away in its own smoke.
And sometime in those meaningful hours, we

who have never found a use for the thing
except to mismanage its name,
as is our bitter nature, did not hear
the hedge apple at last

let go. It left
a little footprint on our hood.
It rolled beneath the less burdened tree, in that darkness—
not a child's forsaken ball, not the body

of a green, malignant thought, neither omen nor even
punishment for our evening's joy,
though we called it so.
It was a hedge apple, only. It was nothing

we would ever hope to hold, in love or burning thirst,
to our parting lips—we
who mistake such things for signs
and for our sustenance,

we who've simply stayed too long.

Starlight

Tonight I skate on adult ankle across the blue pond
sifted with snow, back and forth across ice lit
as if from underneath by moonlight and many stars.
As I sweep and turn, the wind warms itself
inside my collar and rings the cattle's crystal bells
where they huddle over ranging fields. *Starlight*,
she whispers, *bright stars*, though the tiny
woman I have always loved can't see them.

What is it like to drift between your life and your life?
Needles dot her arms, nurses rub their cotton cloths
like clouds across her face. Like melting ice
the fluids drop down trickling to their tubes.
When I take her hand, and off we go, our skates slice
lightly in the rippled ice, her hair blown-frost
and tangled. She tugs my arm and sings *I wish*.
Brittle tree limbs crackle in sudden gusts

and so she leaves me, skating ahead with surprising grace,
called to by something else. Once I watched her
pile of precious scraps become a quilt.
Once she pulled it to my chin and in my first sickness
I kicked it off. The fragile ice, blue-floured ice
we cut across, groans and gives, grows weaker.
Each time we pass in time. Once she wept when
her child's children, sullen in their hand-me-downs,

scuffed early home from school and wouldn't speak.
In this grown place, across blue sheets, we swing
until my ankles tire and ache. Who can finally reach her
where she whips beneath the trees? She pirouettes and floats,
she spins alone in spray, her body lifting luminous and whole
like song, now like a prayer. So this is what we are.

On she glides when I have stopped. On she sails when I have
laid me down and under starlight closed my eyes.

Patriotics

Yesterday a little girl got slapped to death by her daddy,
    out of work, alcoholic, and estranged two towns down river.
America, it's hard to get your attention politely.
    America, the beautiful night is about to blow up

and the cop who brought the man down with a shot to the chops
    is shaking hands, dribbling chaw across his sweaty shirt,
and pointing to cars across the courthouse grass to park.
    It's the Big One one more time, July the 4th,

our country's perfect holiday, so direct a metaphor for war
    we shoot off bombs, launch rockets from Drano cans,
spray the streets and neighbors' yards with the machine-gun crack
    of fireworks, with rebel yells and beer. In short, we celebrate.

It's hard to believe. But so help the soul of Thomas Paine,
    the entire country must be here—the acned faces of neglect,
the halter-tops and ties, the bellies, badges, beehives
    jacked-up cowboy boots, yes, the back-up singers of democracy

all gathered to brighten in unambiguous delight
    when we attack the calm pointless sky. With terrifying vigor
the whistle-stop across the river will lob its smaller arsenal
    halfway back again. Some may be moved to tears.

We'll clean up fast, drive home slow, and tomorrow
    get back to work, those of us with jobs, convicting the others
in the back rooms of our courts and malls—yet what
    will be left of that one poor child, veteran of no war

but her family's own? The comfort of a welfare plot,
    a stalk of wilting prayers? Our fathers' dreams come true as nightmare.
So the first bomb blasts and echoes through the streets and shrubs:
    red, white, and blue sparks shower down, a plague

of patriotic bugs. Our thousand eyeballs burn aglow like punks.

America, I'd swear I don't believe in you, but here I am,
and here you are, and here we stand again, agape.

Running the River Lines

Tonight, on a bank line strung
for catfish, a crawdad hooked through the tail
and dangled scarcely an inch
in the murky water, we catch a loon.

It must have seen our bait, scouting
overhead for something to eat, a school of minnows
or a washed-up mussel to pick apart,
and somehow snagged itself. No wonder

we haven't caught any fish,
the way it flaps there splashing and crying
its hideous cry, hurt
by the small hook at the corner of its beak

but more utterly amazed
that its wings will not bear it away from the bank.
It shrieks and splashes as we draw close,
straining against the willow pole

until it finally rips itself loose, beats its way
low over the water,
lifting at last, disappearing
into the river evening,

its cry still strung between us like a fine line.

The Wrecker Driver Foresees Your Death

I don't drive for pleasure anymore.

If you walked past the lot on any good Sunday,
stopped to stare, and jays were
flying anyway you turned
like blue flowers
tossed up to the wind and rolled over,
so light they never fell,
and the air was fruity with fresh-mown grass,

you could never know the horror of it.
Looking at the rows of cars wrinkled
like wads of paper,
windshields webbed with cracks,
oil still oozing from the fresh ones
hauled in the night before, you still could
not believe the pain. You would try to

hear them collide, perhaps, and might even
convince yourself you could.
You might see the black well of night
crossed with lights flashing
in your mind, or imagine yourself pushing
a stuck door to help the dying
woman crying for you, holding up her damp stub,

the smell of singed hair thick
as honeysuckle, and far sweeter.
For that moment you would stand there
blackhearted, scared of your own mind,
the distant bells and slow
Sunday wind barely discernible,
the birds descending with the shadows,

and you would turn to go, scuffing
through the cut grass, your shoes slick with it.
You could go on like that
swearing to be more careful in your life—
swearing never to drive again,
or never to be so close to people they might die
weeping in your arms, or you in theirs,

each of these a promise you could never keep.

The Anniversary of Silence

May 1972, May 1982

Every night for weeks, from the lilac's deep heart,
a catbird has softly sung through my sleep,
the same one always quietly mewing when I come home
or when I bend beneath it in the garden. This morning
I listened until the bulbs I planted seemed
like teardrops and I put them in the ground sadly.
Once there was a beauty even in the wreckage
we made of the world. The old quarry lake
lay waveless as it freckled under that evening's
early moon, and the low piles of rubble rock
shone along the shore bare in the failing light.
Who could blame us as we stepped out of our clothes

and dove into the green heart of water? Who
could have seen there, like a dim, floating stone
in the still sheen, the ball of cottonmouths simmering?
There was nothing we could do. We stood back
on the glistening bank and watched as she just drifted.
She had found their black secret, so they must have been
on her, mouths blossoming like white flowers,
her mouth open as if to call or sing, yet oddly silent,
perhaps already choked with water. Or perhaps she really
smiled, as it seemed to us who were too far to see
the details of fear, as she floated among them
in the lovely evening, waving to us on the shore.

Every night it has sung softly through my sleep.
Now I lie here restless, alone, tugged
from the slow wash of slumber not by light
or any noise, but by a silence dark and choking.
I do not know whether the bird has flown away or what

has happened. It is too dark to see anything
from the window, except the late wind wasting away
in the nearest leaves, and a few stars high, faint.
How strange to feel such loss at this small
absence. I wish I could reach out and touch her
hand where she floats, and pull her from the darkness.
I wish I heard her singing softly, safe now, saved.

Haunts

Salt Lake deputy sheriffs have identified a skeleton
found above 10,000 feet as that of a hunter reported
missing from his home 27 years ago.
Salt Lake Tribune

In the bleached-bone white
glow of a winter dawn
he has risen
past the old truck road snowed-in
this close to timberline

these months
when hunger drives the herds
of whitetail and elk
down from higher country
and drives the dogged hunters up.

He pauses, hand to trunk
of twisted scrub pine,
puffing hard, a ghost
of breath shredding in the wind:
all this time, and only now

have I seen him
painfully squinting, loaded down
like the young hunter he is,
shells jammed into pockets
like deadly change,

brand new boots,
lugging a 30.30 broken
over his arm and down-pointing
like a dog on scent.
I did not know until now

how far he has come, so early,
slogging like a pilgrim
just to get to Gobbler's Knob,
5000 feet above the Mormon valley
whose schools, today, will be

empty, whole families
stalking deer—only a few,
he knows, will push this high
to where the starving bucks
wander, haunting

the white hills year after year
for less and less.
He touches his gloves
to his face, numb, sweating,
fingers the safety, tries

to focus farther
in the ice-glare of morning sun:
I did not know he has been
with me all this time.
The morning I was born,

the length of a country away
but the same cold
week of his climb,
the Maine snow fell in fistfuls,
my father says. All I felt,

I suppose, was the first chilled
slap of breath at five a.m.
and, later, the draft
of the white room above
the elderly landlady—

how happy she had been
to have a baby boy
in the house once more, and how
surprised: "What?
David? For me?"

my father drawls to tell it.
So she smiled to hold
the child, wrapped
him warm in her thinning quilt,
pressing him to her

as if against the cold days
of her own small life.
The snow packed deeper
into the breaking shapes
of the firs, and she sang

as she rocked him, long
and at last, to sleep.
No one knew then
that a hunger had died in Utah.
No one knew what happened

to the boy until last week
when a skeleton
was found beneath a stand
of scrub pine, high up, Gobbler's Knob,
wallet sodden beneath a generation

of pine needles,
gun stock rotten, safety on.
I see him now, again,
grimly white on the hillside
in the bitter afternoon

as the storm swells, sun gone:
the wind hounds him
and he bends, straining
to breathe the high ice-crust,
though such an echo is plenty

to rouse a deer. But no longer
does he raise his head
to the promise of that distance.
He will not go much farther,
I can tell now. Soon

the snow will whip so hard
he will cry out:
he will surely stumble, weak-
ankled, hurt. There will be nothing
I can do as his face freezes

like a fist. He will just huddle,
beneath a small pine, to rest.
He will try to rub his legs
and remember his name.
He will stay there

finally too cold to shiver,
relaxing, gun on lap,
and look over the beautiful, sweeping
emptiness the world has become,
for all of my life.

Notes

Some of the poems in *Swift* are dedicated to the following people: "Why Not Say" to Donald Dayle Baker; "Waiting for News" to Page Hill Starzinger; "What Is a Weed?," "Never-Ending Birds," and "Hyper-" to Katie Baker; "Scavenger Loop" to Martha Baker; "Late Pastoral" to Linda Gregerson; "Treatise on Touch" to Ann Townsend; "Still-Hildreth Sanitorium, 1936" and "Starlight" to Vesta Fowler; "Running the River Lines" to Tim Gaines.

As a writer lives among people, a poem lives among poems. In addition to quotations I've attributed in my poems—for instance to Emily Dickinson and John Clare—I have reused phrases and information from other sources, as noted:

EPIGRAPH

ix The epigraph to this book is from Edward Taylor's "Huswifery" (*The Poems of Edward Taylor*, Yale University Press, 1960).

NEW POEMS

"Why Not Say"

4 The phrase "why not say what happened" comes from Robert Lowell's "Epilogue" (*Collected Poems*, Farrar, Straus and Giroux, 2007); "there was something deadly in it" is from Brigit Pegeen Kelly's "The Dragon" (*The Orchard*, BOA Editions, 2004).

"Early May"

5 The italic passages are phrases from Elizabeth Kolbert's *The Sixth Extinction: An Unnatural History* (Henry Holt and Company, 2014).

"Stolen Sonnet"

7 The phrase "and stars that fell [just] like [the] rain out of the blue" is from Johnny Mercer's lyrics to "I Remember You" (Sony ATV Music Publishing, 1941); the phrase "which is I stood and loved you while you slept" is from Miller Williams's "A Poem for Emily" (*Some Jazz a While: Collected Poems*, University of Illinois Press, 1999).

"Why Not Say"

9 The phrase "why not say what happened" comes from Robert Lowell's "Epilogue" (*Collected Poems*, Farrar, Straus and Giroux, 1977); the phrase "permanent havoc of little mistakes" is from Linda Gregerson's "An Arbor" (*Prodigal: New and Selected Poems, 1976–2014*, Houghton Mifflin Harcourt, 2015).

"The Sea"

11 The phrase "by means of tiny, transparent, adhesive tube feet" is from an entry, "Sea Urchin," in Wikipedia.

"The Osprey"

14 The phrases in quotation are from "Osprey" in Wikipedia.

"The Wren"

17 The italic phrase is from "Wren" in Wikipedia.

"Checkpoint"

19 "These are the days when Birds come back" is the opening of Emily Dickinson's #122 (*The Poems of Emily Dickinson: Reading Edition*, Harvard University Press, 1999). I have derived some of the immigration questions based on "Could You and Your Partner Pass a U.S. Immigration Marriage Interview?" by Leonora Epstein, *BuzzFeed*, May 7, 2014.

"Peril Sonnet"

22 The opening of my poem echoes the first phrase, "Where do you suppose the moths went," in W. S. Merwin's "Peril" (*Writings to an Unfinished Accompaniment*, Atheneum, 1974).

SCAVENGER LOOP

"Simile"

29 The italic passage is a line from Walt Whitman's "To Think of Time" (*Leaves of Grass and Other Writings*, W. W. Norton & Company, 2002).

"What Is a Weed?"

30 The question "What is a weed?" and my image of the "answerer" derive from Ralph Waldo Emerson's title lecture in *The Fortune of the Republic: And Other American Addresses* (Creative Media Partners, 2015); other information comes from "Emerald Ash Borer," an entry in Wikipedia.

"Magnolia"

33 The phrase "mutinous in [the] half-light, & malignant" is from John Berryman's #12 in "Sonnets to Chris" (*John Berryman: Collected Poems 1937–1971*, Farrar, Straus and Giroux, 1991); "The eye begins to see" is from Theodore Roethke's

"In a Dark Time" (*The Collected Poems of Theodore Roethke*, Anchor Books, 1975); some information comes from "Magnolia," an entry in Wikipedia.

"Five Odes on Absence"

34 The phrase "Because I could not stop for Death" is the first line of Emily Dickinson's #479 (*The Poems of Emily Dickinson: Reading Edition*, Harvard University Press, 1999); the Walker Art Museum quotations are from press information for Erasure Poetry Festival, April 8, 2011; the phrase "Wherever I am I am what is missing" is from Mark Strand's "Keeping Things Whole" (*Collected Poems,* Knopf, 2014).

Among John Clare's late letters, written during his long residency at the Northampton General Lunatic Asylum, was a draft of a letter to a Mary Collingwood. Clare wrote this letter in code—a simple erasure of vowels and the letter "y." Jonathan Bate reckons that Clare may have used code to protect his privacy in case someone was going through his notebooks. Or, Bate continues, "the disappearance of the vowels may have been a step on the road to the later mental degeneration that led him to speak of how his head had been cut off" (*John Clare: A Biography*, Farrar, Straus and Giroux, 2003).

My poem includes the following phrases from Clare's letter. After each phrase I present here its likely meaning, according to Bate: *M Drst . . . M nrl wrn t* / My Dearest . . . I am nearly worn out. *Nbd wll wn M r hv m . . . & wht hv dn . . .* / Nobody will own (want?) me or have me . . . and what have I done. *ppl tll m hv gt n hm n ths wrld . . .* / People tell me I have got no home in this world. *Drst Mr r fthfll r d thnk f m . . . dd vst me n hll sm tm bck . . . flsh ppl tll m hv gt n hm n ths wrld . . .* / Dearest Mary are you faithful or do you think of me . . . you did visit me in hell sometime back . . . foolish people tell me I have got no home in this world. *whr r th* / Where are they? *bt dnt cm hr gn fr t s ntrs bd plc . . . rs fr vr & vr Jhn Clr* / But don't come here again for it is a notorious bad place . . . yours for ever and ever John Clare.

I reprint several lines from a manuscript draft of Clare's long poem, "October," part of his *The Shepherd's Calendar*. The cross-outs and revisions are Clare's. I quote passages from two other Clare poems that Bate identifies as "Lines: 'I Am'" and "Sonnet: 'I Am.'" My quotations from Clare's poems come from Jonathan Bate's edited volume, *I Am: The Selected Poetry of John Clare* (Farrar, Straus and Giroux, 2003).

"Belong To"

39 The phrases "Raining and morning," "the first soft ashes," "like coals," and "all the muffled horns" come from Mary Ruefle's "All the Activity There Is" (*Selected Poems*, Wave Books, 2010). The final italic phrase is from Franz Wright's "Old Story" (*Walking to Martha's Vineyard*, Knopf, 2003).

"Scavenger Loop"

41 I have rummaged through many other writers' works to compose this sequence. Of particular inspiration has been Bernd Heinrich's work, especially *Life Everlasting: The Animal Way of Death* (Houghton Mifflin Harcourt,

2012). I quote four passages from his book, identified here with the beginning with each passage: "In the wild, animals lie where they die"; "More than a third of the bird species"; "We deny that we are animals"; "The amount of fossil fuel required."

The passage on *Dustscaewung* is from Melanie Challenger's book *On Extinction: How We Become Estranged from Nature* (Counterpoint, 2012). "Something is coming more than we know how" is a line in Frederick Seidel's "Green Absinthe" (*Widening Income Inequality*, Farrar, Straus and Giroux, 2016). The passage beginning "The USDA projected 2013 US corn production" is from Ron Sterk's online article "Outlook Positive for Most Crops" (*Food Business News*, May 21, 2013). The passage beginning "When we reduce biodiversity by breaking up" is from Richard Conniff's online article "What Are Species Worth?" (*Yale Environment 360*, Sept. 27, 2010). The line "You may not be tired but I'm tired" is from Louise Glück's "First Snow" (*A Village Life*, Farrar, Straus and Giroux, 2009). Two lines beginning "Come, kill the Worm" are from Edward Taylor's "Preparatory Meditations," First Series, #49 (*The Poems of Edward Taylor*, Yale University Press, 1960). "Who would I show it to" is from W. S. Merwin's "Elegy" (*The Second Four Books of Poems*, Copper Canyon Press, 1993). The line beginning "The world gives you itself" is from Mario Santiago Papasquiaro's *Advice from 1 Disciple of Marx to 1 Heidegger Fanatic* (Wave Books, 2013). The four lines beginning "The grey lawns cold" are from Gerard Manley Hopkins's "The Starlight Night" (*Gerard Manley Hopkins: A Critical Edition of the Major Works*, Oxford University Press, 1986). I adapt three phrases from Margaret Wise Brown's *Goodnight Moon* (HarperCollins Publishers, 2007). "The world is full of prayers arrived at from afterwards" is from W. S. Merwin's "Words from a Totem Animal" (*The Second Four Books of Poems*, Copper Canyon Press, 1993). The phrase starting "Tell me your relation to pain" is from Ernst Junger's *On Pain* (Telos Press, 2008). The two lines starting "I am looking at trees" are from W. S. Merwin's "Trees" (*The Compass Flower*, Atheneum, 1977). "Cover her when she sleeps" is from Brenda Hillman's "Light Galaxies Sleep for Our Mother" (*Seasonal Works with Letters on Fire*, Wesleyan, 2009). The passage beginning "But trees do not dwell" is from Colin Tudge's *The Tree* (Crown Publishers, 2006). Information about Monsanto's corn worm product comes from their online news release, "Genuity Smartstax RIB Complete Corn Blend Delivers Full-Season Corn Rootworm Control" (April 16, 2012). A few lines and passages from my own previous work are woven into this sequence.

NEVER-ENDING BIRDS

"Posthumous Man"

75 Passages about John Keats derive from his poems "Ode to a Nightingale" and "Ode to Psyche," as well as from his letter of July 25, 1819, to Fanny Brawne, and his famous last letter to Charles Brown, on November 30, 1820, in which he writes, "I have an habitual feeling of my real life having past,

and that I am leading a posthumous existence." These poems and letters are from *John Keats: A Critical Edition of the Major Works* (Oxford University Press, 1990).

"Horse Madness"

82 The detail about the eyes of goats and sheep comes from A. Rodger Ekirch's *At Day's Close: Night in Times Past* (W. W. Norton & Company, 2006). Other images and phrases, including my title phrase, "horse madness," derive from *The Georgics of Virgil: Bilingual Edition* (trans. David Ferry, Farrar, Straus and Giroux, 2005).

MIDWEST ECLOGUE

"Midwest Eclogue"

101 The question from Corydon is from Virgil's Eclogue II, as Corydon, chiding himself, sings of his hopeless love of Alexis. The last sentence of my poem is from Virgil's Eclogue I, as Tityrus concludes his first dialogue with Meliboeus. These come from *The Eclogues of Virgil: Bilingual Edition* (trans. David Ferry, Farrar, Straus and Giroux, 1999).

THE TRUTH ABOUT SMALL TOWNS

"Tract"

137 The epigraph is from a journal entry by Ralph Waldo Emerson, dated April 26, 1838, as he reflected on his letter to President Van Buren, protesting "the removal of the Cherokee Indians from the State of Georgia." Emerson's entry appears in *The Journals and Miscellaneous Notebooks of Ralph Waldo Emerson*, vol. 5, 1835–1838 (Harvard University Press, 1965).

"Treatise on Touch"

140 The italic passage beginning "Divine I am inside and out" is from section 24 of Walt Whitman's "Song of Myself" (*Leaves of Grass and Other Writings*, W. W. Norton & Company, 2002); the italic passage beginning "The rays that come from heavenly worlds" is from Ralph Waldo Emerson's "Nature" (*Selections from Ralph Waldo Emerson*, Houghton Mifflin Company, 1957). I have configured these passages into my syllabic structure.